Contents

How to use this book

Start by writing your name on the front cover – this workbook has been designed for you!

You can use it as you progress through your GCSE Religious Studies course, or as part of your revision for the final exam. It's full of different activities to help you learn by doing, not just reading.

This workbook covers the study of Christianity and Buddhism for Paper 1.

This refers to pages in these student books. Chapters 1 and 2 refer to the Christianity book. Chapters 4 and 5 refer to the Buddhism book. You can go back to your student books to read about the topic in more depth.

Activity

SB pages 2–3

Working your way through these activities will help strengthen your understanding of some of the key topics in your GCSE course.

Follow the instructions and write your answers in the space provided.

_____

_____

_____

Challenge activity

SB pages 2–3

If you really want to stretch yourself, have a go at these challenge activities.

_____

_____

_____

There are lots of blank lines for you to write in your answers.

Key terms

SB pages 2–3

It's important to get to grips with some of the specialist language that we use when talking about religion. You will need to recognise these 'key terms' because they may turn up in an exam question. And you will also need to know how to use them in your answers. These activities will help you to feel confident using religious language. Test yourself regularly on these terms.

Key Terms Glossaries appear at the end of chapters 1, 2, 4 and 5.

Key Terms Glossary _____

You can collect the meanings of key terms here so you can refer to them at any time. You will also be creating a useful revision tool.

Sources of religious belief and teaching

 pages 2–3

The 5-mark question in the exam asks you to 'refer to scripture or another source of Christian/Buddhist belief and teaching.' These activities will help you to memorise short quotations from religious sources, such as the Bible or the Dhammapada, and also explain what these quotations mean.

This will also be helpful for the 4-mark and 12-mark questions because you can refer to religious teachings to add detail to the points you make, and to back up your arguments.

TIP

Keep an eye out for these TIPS. They contain useful advice, especially to help with your exam.

Exam practice

If you see an arrow running down the side of a box, that means the activity or activities you are doing will end with an exam practice question. These are like the questions that you will encounter in your exams. Use the information and guidance from the activities to practise the 1, 2, 4, 5 and 12-mark questions.

Finally, there are two whole chapters dedicated to

Exam practice

There are five different types of question in the AQA exam paper – the **1, 2, 4, 5** and **12-mark** questions.

Work your way through this chapter to find out what each question will look like and how it is marked.

There are some activities that will help you to understand what the examiner is looking for in an answer, and activities that practise the skills you should be demonstrating. You should then be ready to have a go at a few questions yourself.

WHAT WILL THE QUESTION LOOK LIKE?

This explains the command words that the question will use.

HOW IS IT MARKED?

This explains what the examiner will be looking for in your answer.

 REMEMBER...

This provides useful tips to help raise your marks.

All answers can be found online at **www.oxfordsecondary.co.uk/aqa-rs-answers**, so you can mark what you've done.

Once you have filled out this workbook, you will have made your own book to revise from. That's why your name is on the cover.

Chapter 1: Christianity: Beliefs and teachings

Activity 1.1: Monotheism expressed in the Bible

S B page 9

Monotheism consists of two main beliefs:

- **Mono**, which refers to belief in only one God

- **Theism**, which refers to belief in a personal God who created and sustains the world, and who is active within it.

These beliefs are expressed in this quotation:

> **"** I am the LORD your God, **who brought you out of Egypt**, out of the land of slavery. You shall **have no other gods** before me. **"**
>
> *Exodus* 20:2–3

Shows God is a personal being who is active in the world

Shows Christians should only worship one God

TIP

These page references refer to the Christianity Student Book.

Two more quotations are given below. For each one, explain how the quotation expresses the idea of monotheism, i.e. the idea that there is only one God, or that God created the world and is active within it.

TIP

When you are learning quotations, always make sure you know how they relate to a belief.

> **"** We believe in one God, the Father, the Almighty, maker of heaven and earth, of all that is, seen and unseen. **"**
>
> *Nicene Creed*

_____

_____

_____

_____

> **"** For you created my inmost being; you knit me together in my mother's womb. **"**
>
> *Psalm* 139:13

_____

_____

_____

_____

Activity 1.2: How monotheism influences Christians today   (S B)   **page 9**

A How does a belief in monotheism influence Christians today? Tick the **two** statements that you think are most likely.

It leads to a person being fully committed to Christianity and no other faith. ☐

It means a Christian does not fear death. ☐

It means a Christian trusts God as they know everything is in his power. ☐

It leads to a Christian reading the Bible on a regular basis. ☐

It leads to a Christian praying to God as they know he listens and cares. ☐

> **TIP**
> Remember that monotheism is a belief in only one God who is active within the world. Which two statements do you think are most connected to this belief?

B Explain why you chose these two statements.

_____

_____

_____

_____

_____

Exam practice

Use your answers to the previous two activities to answer this exam question.

Explain **two** ways in which a belief in monotheism influences Christians today.   **[4 marks]**

_____

_____

_____

_____

_____

_____

_____

_____

_____

> **TIP**
> Your answer needs to focus on how monotheism affects Christians today. How does monotheism influence how they act or what they think? Remember to make two points and develop each one with detail. This could be an example or a quote.

Activity 1.3: God as loving

 pages 10–11

In the Bible, love is described as 'patient', 'kind' and 'not self-seeking'. It 'always protects, always trusts, always hopes, always perseveres. Love never fails.' (*1 Corinthians* 13:7-8). Jesus explains how this relates to the benevolent or all-loving nature of God through the Parable of the Good Samaritan.

A Read this summary of the Parable of the Good Samaritan.

One day a man was walking down a dangerous road when he was beaten and left seriously injured. Two other men (one of whom was a priest) passed him by rather than stopping to help. But a Samaritan, who was a stranger and a person from an enemy land, came down the road. He saw the injured man and was moved with pity. Despite the fact that he too could be attacked, the Samaritan cleaned and bandaged his wounds, put him on his donkey, and took him to an inn where he took care of the injured man. The next day he gave the innkeeper some money to look after the injured man, as he had to go to work.

B Now explain how the parable shows the different qualities of love (as identified in *1 Corinthians*). How does the parable show that love is not self-seeking, but protecting and persevering?

> **TIP**
> 'Self-seeking' means putting concern for yourself before other people.

The idea that love is not self-seeking is shown when:

_____

_____

_____

_____

_____

The idea that love protects is shown when:

_____

_____

_____

_____

_____

The idea that love perseveres and does not give up is shown when:

_____

_____

_____

_____

_____

Activity 1.4: God acting in a loving way

 pages 10–11

In Christianity, the love of God is key to understanding all of God's other attributes. For example, God is also said to be omnipotent and just, but he expresses these qualities in a loving way.

Below are three actions carried out by God. Use the left-hand column of the table to explain how God carries out these actions in a loving way. Then use the right-hand column of the table to explain how God could carry out these actions in a non-loving way. One example has been completed for you.

Shows God doing this in a loving way	Action	If God was not loving, this might have meant...
	Creation of the world	
God created humans with free will, so they could choose whether they wanted to have faith in him.	Creation of humans	God could have made humans so they had no choices and just did whatever he wanted.
	Judging humans	

Activity 1.5: Answering a 2-mark question

 pages 10–11

Three students have written different answers to the exam question, 'Give **two** Christian beliefs about the nature of God'. Which answer do you think is the best?

Student A	Student B	Student C
Christians believe God is all loving, which is shown when he created the world. They also believe God is just, which is shown on Judgement day.	God is benevolent. God is all loving.	God is all loving. God is one (monotheism).

The student who wrote the best answer is:

_____

This is because:

_____

_____

_____

_____

> **TIP**
>
> Remember that for a 2-mark question, you need to make two **separate** points. You don't need to waste time by giving extra explanation – short, **simple** answers are fine.

Challenge activity 1.6: The Trinity

 pages 12–13

Christians believe all three persons of the Trinity are fully and equally God.

A The pictures below are trying to illustrate the concept of the Trinity. Complete the table to show which picture you think works best. Explain your reasons, and also explain why you think the others are not as good as the one you have chosen.

	Which picture works best and why? Why are the others not as good?
○ ○ ○	
⊕⊕⊕	

⊕ (three overlapping circles diagram)	
⊕ (three overlapping circles diagram)	

B Explain why the Trinity is important in Christianity.

_____

_____

_____

_____

_____

_____

_____

_____

C How could it be argued that the mystery of the Trinity is not helpful in enabling a Christian to have a personal relationship with God?

_____

_____

_____

_____

_____

_____

_____

TIP

Having a personal relationship with someone means you have to know who they are. Can this happen with God if no one can really understand who he is?

Key terms

pages 12–15

In the statements below, decide which of the key terms could replace the phrase that has been written in bold.

Genesis	benevolence		omnipotence	literal
Trinity	Out of nothing (*ex nihilo* in Latin)		Creator	symbolic

TIP

Try to use correct religious words in your answers to exam questions. It will allow you to express yourself more accurately, and it shows the examiner you have a good understanding of key vocabulary.

1. Christians believe that God is the **maker of everything in the universe**.

Key term

2. Christians believe God's **loving nature** is shown in his creation of the world, as he created everything to be 'very good'.

Key term

3. Some Christians reject scientific accounts of creation as they believe only a **word for word** account of the biblical stories should be followed.

Key term

4. Christians believe the **three persons of God** was present at creation. For example, Genesis says: 'the Spirit of God was hovering over the waters'.

Key term

5. Christians believe the creation of the world shows the omnipotence of God because he created this **by not using anything at all**.

Key term

6. The account of creation is described in **the first book of the Bible**.

Key term

Sources of religious belief and teaching

 pages 16–17

Read the quotation below and answer the questions that follow.

> **❝The Word became flesh and made his dwelling among us.❞**
> *John* 1:14

This quotation expresses the belief of the incarnation: when God took on human form and became Jesus.

1. Who is John referring to when he talks about 'the Word'?

   _____

2. What does 'the Word became flesh' mean?

   _____

   _____

   _____

3. For Christians, this quotation shows that Jesus was fully God. Why is it important to Christians that Jesus was not just an ordinary human being?

   _____

   _____

   _____

   _____

   _____

Activity 1.7: Jesus as fully human and fully God

 pages 16–17

Read the summary below about Jesus' birth, life and death. Using one colour, highlight any events which show that Jesus was fully God. Then using another colour, highlight any events which show that Jesus was fully human.

Mary, a young woman living in Nazareth, was visited by an angel who told her that she was going to become pregnant through the Holy Spirit. This means that Joseph was not the biological father of Jesus.

Mary gave birth to Jesus naturally. After his birth, Jesus was visited by shepherds and wise men who had become aware that a Messiah or saviour had been born. When Jesus was a baby, Mary and Joseph took him to the Temple and a priest there recognised Jesus as God's Messiah or saviour. After this, most of Jesus' early life was spent in Nazareth, learning his father's trade as a carpenter and taking part in Jewish religious activities.

When he was in his early 30s, Jesus was baptised by his cousin John. During his baptism, a voice from heaven said 'You are my Son'. After this event, Jesus spent the next few years spreading the message of God and performing miracles. Significant miracles included bringing people back from the dead. There are also accounts of when he was worried (such as just before his arrest) and when he did not know everything (such as when the disciples asked him when the Day of Judgement would be). Christians believe that Jesus ascended to heaven after he was resurrected, where he sits on the right hand of the Father.

Activity 1.8: Key beliefs linked to Jesus' crucifixion pages 16–19

Christians believe that Jesus' crucifixion demonstrates the following four key beliefs:

1. Jesus was fully God

2. Jesus was fully human

3. It was part of God's plan that Jesus would die and ascend to heaven

4. Jesus' behaviour while he was crucified demonstrates how Christians should respond to suffering

Look at the four quotations below. Identify which of the four key beliefs above links to each quotation. Then explain how each quotation helps illustrate this key belief.

Quotation	Which belief does this relate to? How does the quotation illustrate this belief?
To the people who caused him to suffer, Jesus said: **❝Father, forgive them, for they do not know what they are doing. ❞** *Luke* 23:34	
A criminal being crucified next to Jesus said: **❝ Jesus, remember me when you come into your kingdom. Jesus answered him, 'Truly I tell you, today you will be with me in paradise.' ❞** *Luke* 23:42–3	
Jesus suffered so much on the cross that at one point he cried out: **❝My God, my God, why have you forsaken me? ❞** *Mark* 15:34	
After witnessing the crucifixion, a Roman centurion said: **❝Surely this man was the Son of God! ❞** *Mark* 15:39	

Activity 1.9: The death, resurrection and ascension of Jesus pages 18–21

The following events are connected to the death, resurrection and ascension of Jesus but they are not in the correct order. Put them in the correct order in the table below.

A	After some time, Jesus ascends into heaven.
B	Peter is informed that Jesus has been resurrected. The other disciples are also informed.
C	Early Friday morning, Jesus is tried by the Jewish council (called the Sanhedrin) and by the Roman Governor (Pontius Pilate).
D	Late on Thursday evening, Jesus is arrested in the Garden of Gethsemane.
E	Early Sunday morning, Mary Magdalene (and perhaps other women) discover the tomb is empty.
F	The resurrected Jesus appears to different disciples.
G	Jesus is crucified along with two other people. He dies around 3 in the afternoon on the Friday.
H	On Thursday evening, Jesus celebrates the Last Supper with his disciples.
I	Jesus' body is placed in the tomb on Friday evening before the Jewish Sabbath begins.

The correct order is:

1:	2:	3:	4:	5:	6:	7:	8:	9:

Exam practice

Now answer the following exam question.

Give **two** Christian beliefs about Jesus' crucifixion.   **[2 marks]**

1 _____

_____

2 _____

_____

TIP
Remember that for a 2-mark question you only need to write two simple points.

Activity 1.10: The evidence for Jesus' resurrection

 pages 20–21

There are six pieces of evidence below that could be used to support the belief that Jesus was resurrected. Select the **two** pieces of evidence that you think a Christian would more likely use to support their belief that Jesus was resurrected. Write your choices in the space below and give reasons for your answer. Then explain why someone might disagree with this evidence.

Evidence A:
There were many witnesses to Jesus' resurrection, as he appeared to different people many times after his death.

Evidence B:
Jesus is the Son of God, therefore nothing is impossible for him as he is omnipotent.

Evidence C:
It was always God's plan for Jesus to be resurrected, as this shows it is possible for humans to survive death as well.

Evidence D:
Jesus said: 'The Son of Man must suffer many things … be killed and on the third day be raised to life.' (*Luke* 9:22)

Evidence E:
The resurrection is the only possible explanation for the empty tomb, which was confirmed by the angels.

Evidence F:
The Bible says the resurrection happened. The Bible would not contain false information. Therefore it must be true.

TIP

Even if you do not agree with the evidence given here, try to consider which arguments would be most persuasive to a Christian.

My first choice is: _____

This is because: _____

_____

_____

_____

Someone might disagree with this evidence because: _____

_____

_____

_____

My second choice is: _____

This is because: _____

_____

_____

_____

Someone might disagree with this evidence because: _____

_____

_____

_____

Challenge activity 1.11: Jesus' resurrection in the Bible

pages 20–21

The resurrection of Jesus is described in all four of the gospels (*Matthew* 28, *Mark* 16, *Luke* 24 and *John* 20–21).

A In the Bible, the gospel writers made it very clear that Jesus had definitely died. Why do you think they did this?

_____

_____

_____

_____

_____

_____

B The gospel writers also made it clear that the women knew which tomb Jesus had been placed in. Why do you think they stressed this?

_____

_____

_____

_____

_____

_____

_____

_____

TIP

To help you answer these questions, think about how important Jesus' resurrection is to Christian belief.

Exam practice

Now answer this exam question.

Which **one** of the following refers to the belief that Jesus was brought back to life after he died?

[1 mark]

Put a tick (✔) in the box next to the correct answer.

A Ascension ☐

B Resurrection ☐

C Atonement ☐

D Incarnation ☐

Activity 1.12: The significance of Jesus' resurrection

pages 20–23

A Here are three arguments for and three arguments against the statement, 'The resurrection is the most significant event in the story of Jesus'. In the table below, put a tick (✓) in the corner of the arguments that support the statement. Then put a cross (✗) in the corner of the arguments that oppose the statement.

Argument 1

The resurrection is most significant because it proves that Jesus was truly the Son of God.

Argument 2

Jesus' sermons and teachings are more important as they teach people how to avoid sinning in the first place.

Argument 3

The resurrection is most significant as it shows that if a person has faith in Jesus then they can go to heaven when they die.

Argument 4

Jesus' resurrection was significant because it means that humans can now receive forgiveness from God for their sins.

Argument 5

The crucifixion is crucial as it was through this act that Jesus suffered the punishment necessary for sin to be overcome, which is what allows people to go to heaven when they die.

Argument 6

The miracles that Jesus performed when he was alive are just as significant as these also prove that Jesus was fully God.

B Which **one** of these arguments do you think is the strongest (either for or against the statement)? Explain why.

_____

_____

_____

_____

_____

C Consider the arguments above to decide whether you agree or disagree with the statement, 'The resurrection is the most significant event in the story of Jesus'. Then explain your reasoning below to help you reach a justified conclusion.

I agree/disagree with the statement because:

_____

_____

_____

_____

Someone might disagree/agree with this statement because:

_____

_____

_____

_____

TIP

Remember, you are not giving your opinion, but making a judgement based on the evidence presented in the arguments.

Challenge activity 1.13: Paul's description of the resurrection

 pages 22–23

The passage below shows the Christian belief that all people will be resurrected after they die. Here, Paul describes what this resurrected state will be like.

> ❝So will it be with the resurrection of the dead. The body that is sown is perishable, it is raised imperishable; it is sown in dishonour, it is raised in glory; it is sown in weakness, it is raised in power; it is sown a natural body, it is raised a spiritual body. If there is a natural body, there is also a spiritual body. ❞
>
> *1 Corinthians* 15:42–44

A In the table below, write in the features that Paul says belong to the sown or earthly body (when a person is still alive), and the features that belong to the raised or resurrected body (after a person dies).

The earthly body (The sown body)	The resurrected body (The raised body)

B Explain in your own words what the resurrected body will be like.

_____

_____

_____

C Some Christians (such as Catholics) believe the resurrected body will be a glorified *physical* body rather than a glorified *spiritual* body. Why do you think they believe this?

_____

_____

_____

_____

TIP

Think about whether Jesus' resurrection was physical or spiritual.

D The passage compares the earthly body to a seed that is 'sown', and the resurrected body to a plant that is 'raised' from the ground. What do you think Paul is trying to show with this comparison? How does it help a Christian to compare the relationship between an earthly body and a resurrected body?

_____

_____

_____

_____

Activity 1.14: Christian beliefs about the afterlife

pages 24–27

The following terms relate to Christian beliefs about the afterlife. Connect pairs of terms to write four sentences about Christian attitudes to the afterlife. For example:

*Christians believe the **love** of **God** makes the afterlife possible.*

If you wish, you can use a term more than once.

Judgement	love	God	eternal life	Jesus
serving others	resurrected	heaven	faith	purgatory

1 _____

_____

2 _____

_____

3 _____

_____

4 _____

_____

Activity 1.15: Receiving a favourable judgement from God

pages 24–25

Many Christians believe that in order to be judged favourably by God, they need to:

1. Serve and help those in need

2. Have faith in Jesus.

In the table below, give **three** examples of the activities a Christian could perform to fulfil both criteria. Try to link these examples to specific practices found within Christianity if you can.

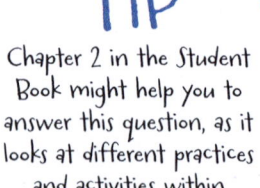

TIP

Chapter 2 in the Student Book might help you to answer this question, as it looks at different practices and activities within Christianity.

Christians should...	To show this in their lives, Christians could...
Serve those in need (see the Parable of the Sheep and Goats in *Matthew* 25:31–36)	1 _____ _____ _____ 2 _____ _____ _____

	3 _____ _____ _____ _____
Accept that Jesus is the Son of God and follow his teachings (see Jesus' reply to the disciple Thomas in *John* 14:6)	1 _____ _____ _____ _____ 2 _____ _____ _____ _____ 3 _____ _____ _____ _____

Exam practice

Use your answers to Activity 1.15 to answer the following exam question.

Explain **two** Christian teachings about Judgement.

Refer to sacred writings or another source of Christian belief and teaching in your answer.   **[5 marks]**

_____

_____

_____

_____

_____

_____

_____

_____

_____

_____

_____

_____

Activity 1.16: Divergent views of heaven and hell

  pages 26–27

A The first column of the table below gives examples of Christian views on heaven and hell. Colour in blue the views connected to heaven, and colour in red the views connected to hell.

B In the second column of the table, draw a cross (**X**) somewhere along the shaded rectangle depending on how strongly you think Christians agree with this interpretation of heaven or hell.

For example, draw a cross towards 'Agree' if you think nearly all Christians agree with this interpretation of heaven or hell. Draw a cross towards 'Disagree' if you think there is strong disagreement amongst Christians about whether this is really what heaven or hell is like.

> **TIP**
>
> Some Christians disagree about whether descriptions of heaven and hell are literal or symbolic. For example, is hell really full of fire and flames, or does this imagery symbolise the absence of God?

Views of heaven and hell	Do Christians agree with this view of heaven or hell?	
Fire and flames	Agree	Disagree
Presence of God	Agree	Disagree
Perfect and good	Agree	Disagree
Eternal	Agree	Disagree
Ruled by the Devil	Agree	Disagree
Pain and suffering	Agree	Disagree
For Christians only	Agree	Disagree
Clouds and angels	Agree	Disagree
Absence of God	Agree	Disagree

C Do you think it matters that there are different opinions about heaven and hell in Christianity? Explain your answer.

_____

_____

_____

_____

_____

_____

_____

_____

_____

Activity 1.17: Beliefs about heaven and hell   pages 26–27

For the 4, 5 and 12-mark questions in your exam, it is important that you develop the points you make. Four of the sentences in the boxes below make a point about a Christian view of the afterlife, and four of the sentences develop these points. Identify which point goes with which development by writing them out in the table below.

A loving God would not want to punish people for eternity.	Christians believe God is perfectly just and fair.	Hell would refer to what it is like to have no God or love or goodness in your life.	Jesus shows this when he describes hell as a place of flames and suffering.
Descriptions of hell and heaven refer to states of mind not real places.	True justice can be gained by rewarding the good in heaven and punishing the bad in hell.	The Bible describes heaven and hell as being real places.	C. S. Lewis believed that people in hell have a chance to redeem themselves and transfer to heaven.

Point	Development

Exam practice

Use your answers to the previous two activities to answer this exam question.

'All Christians have the same beliefs about heaven and hell.'
Evaluate this statement.

In your answer you should:

- refer to Christian teaching
- give reasoned arguments to support this statement
- reasoned arguments to support a different point of view
- reach a justified conclusion.

[12 marks]
[SPaG 3 marks]

TIP
Always have at least three paragraphs in your answer. One paragraph should focus on supporting the question and the other should look at arguments against. The final paragraph should be your justified conclusion.

Activity 1.18: Sin and salvation

 pages 28–29

In each of the boxes below there are three religious terms connected to sin and salvation. Explain how these terms are linked to each other, using all three terms in your explanation. One example has been done for you.

Religious terms	How these are connected to each other
sin salvation God	*Christians believe that **salvation** is necessary in order to save people from **sin** and allow them to get close to **God** again. .*
Adam and Eve original sin sin	
Garden of Eden tree of the knowledge of good and evil Satan (the Devil)	
free will God Ten Commandments	
salvation good works grace	

Activity 1.19: The role of Christ in salvation

 pages 28–31

Answer the following questions about the role of Christ in salvation.

1. Explain the difference between original sin and sin.

_____

_____

_____

_____

_____

2. Explain the difference between atonement and salvation.

_____

_____

_____

_____

_____

3. In the Garden of Eden, Adam and Eve ate the fruit from the tree of the knowledge of good and evil. How did this affect the relationship between God and humans?

_____

_____

_____

4. At the end of his life Jesus willingly died on the cross. How did this affect the relationship between God and humans?

_____

_____

> **❝** For since death came through a man, the resurrection of the dead comes also through a man. For as in Adam all die, so in Christ all will be made alive. **❞**
>
> _1 Corinthians_ 15:21–22

5. In your own words, explain what the quotation above means. How does this link to ideas of original sin and salvation?

_____

_____

_____

_____

_____

Key Terms Glossary

As you progress through the course, you can collect the meanings of useful terms in the glossary below. You can then use the completed glossaries to revise from.

To do well in the exam you will need to understand these terms and include them in your answers. Tick the shaded circles to record how confident you feel. Use the extra boxes at the end to record any other terms that you have found difficult, along with their definitions.

- ○ **I recognise this term**
- ◐ **I understand what this term means**
- ● **I can use this term in a sentence**

Afterlife

Ascension

Atonement

Christ

Creation

Crucifixion

Evil

The Father

Grace

Heaven

Hell

Holy Spirit

Omnipotent

Incarnation

Oneness of God

Judgement

Original sin

Just

Resurrection

Law

Salvation

Loving

Sin

Son of God

Suffering

Trinity

The Word

Chapter 2: **Christianity: Practices**

  pages 36–37

Read through the situations below and decide which of the following forms of worship each one best describes: **liturgical**, **non-liturgical**, **informal** or **private worship**. Then explain what the benefits of this type of worship are. One has been done for you as an example.

> We believe that we should try to copy the first disciples and those in the early church. We will meet together in someone's house and discuss what it means to be a Christian. We always try to support each other. There may be prayers, singing and sometimes we have a communal meal. I really feel part of something special.
> Abebe

This is an example of:
Informal worship.

The benefits of this are:
Christians feel they are copying what the earliest Christians were doing. They also feel that they are being supported by other members of the group.

> Every morning I like to read a passage from the Bible. I will spend the rest of the day thinking about how this passage applies to my daily life. I try to make sure I act on this if I can. I find this really helps me to renew my faith each day and to see how it is relevant. If I struggle to do this, I find prayer helps.
> Mary

This is an example of:

The benefits of this are:

> Every Sunday I go to church. Each week we follow the order of service which is printed on a sheet. This tells us when to sing and what prayers to say. The priest gives a sermon and also the Eucharist. I like this way of worshipping as I know I am doing what God wants me to do and I can show him my thanks.
> Paul

This is an example of:

The benefits of this are:

> It is always a bit different but I know that there will be readings from the Bible and our pastor will explain these in a sermon. We often sing hymns and some weeks we celebrate the Eucharist. I like this way of worshipping as it means our pastor can change things according to what we need. It has the personal touch.
> Isabella

This is an example of:

The benefits of this are:

Activity 2.2: The Lord's Prayer

 pages 38–39

Answer the following questions about prayer.

Prayer can be said for many reasons. Some of these reasons can be summarised through the acronym PACT which is:

Praising and adoring God: Christians pray in order to praise and show their adoration of God, reminding themselves of who he is and what he has done.

Asking: Christians may pray to ask God for help or guidance.

Confession: Christians may pray to God in order to say sorry and to ask for forgiveness.

Thanksgiving: Christians may pray to thank God for what he has given them.

1. The Lord's Prayer is a popular prayer used by Christians because it was the way that Jesus told his disciples to pray. Read through the prayer below and identify where there are examples of PACT. Label a line in the prayer with the letters 'P', 'A', 'C' or 'T' to show this (you may not need to use all of these letters). One has been done for you as an example.

   " _P___ Our Father in heaven, hallowed be your name,

   _____ your Kingdom come, your will be done, / on earth as it is in heaven.

   _____ Give us today our daily bread.

   _____ Forgive us our sins / as we forgive those who sin against us.

   _____ Lead us not into temptation, but deliver us from evil.

   _____ For the kingdom, the power, and the glory are yours / now and forever. Amen. "

   > **TIP**
   > Look again at Chapter 1 in the Christianity Student Book, particularly pages 18–19 and 30–31.

2. Why do you think this prayer stresses that a Christian should not only ask God to forgive their sins but that they should also try to forgive those who have sinned against them?

   _____

   _____

   _____

   _____

3. Prayer helps a Christian to accept the will of God. How do you think the Lord's Prayer could do this? In your answer try to include specific words or phrases from the prayer.

   _____

   _____

   _____

   _____

4. Is the Lord's Prayer a set prayer or an informal prayer?

   _____

Activity 2.3: The sacraments

pages 40–41

A Mark the following statements about the sacraments as true or false.

True False

A sacrament is a holy ritual or rite, which many Christians believe is an outward sign of the inner gift of God's love or grace. ☐ ☐

Catholics and Quakers believe there are seven sacraments. ☐ ☐

Baptists and Pentecostal Christians consider believers' baptism to be an important practice but not a sacrament. ☐ ☐

Confirmation, reconciliation and atonement are three of the seven sacraments. ☐ ☐

Protestants celebrate Baptism and Holy Communion. ☐ ☐

Many Christians see baptism as a way for a person to join the Christian church. ☐ ☐

The sacraments help a Christian to strengthen their relationship with God. ☐ ☐

B For the statements you have marked as 'false', write one or two sentences with the correct information.

_____

_____

_____

_____

Activity 2.4: Answering a 4-mark question on baptism

pages 40–41

A student has written an answer to the exam question 'Explain **two** contrasting examples of baptism'. Develop the points below so the answer will gain all 4 marks.

Catholic and Orthodox Christians baptise children. _____

_____

_____

Baptist and Pentecostal Christians do not baptise children. _____

_____

_____

TIP
The 4-mark question in the 'Practices' section of the exam paper will always ask you to give a contrasting point. This contrast does not have to be a completely opposite practice – it could just be a different practice.

Sources of religious belief and teaching

 pages 42–43

A Read the following quotations from the Bible connected to Christian beliefs about Holy Communion.

> **A** "Whoever eats my flesh and drinks my blood has eternal life, and I will raise them up at the last day."
>
> *John 6:54*

> **B** "Whoever eats my flesh and drinks my blood remains in me, and I in them."
>
> *John 6:56*

> **C** "Because there is one loaf, we, who are many, are one body, for we all share the one loaf."
>
> *1 Corinthians 10:17*

> **D** "Jesus took bread… gave it to his disciples, saying, 'Take and eat; this is my body'. Then he took a cup and… he gave it to them saying, 'Drink from it, all of you for this is my blood."
>
> *Matthew 26:26–8*

> **E** "The Lord Jesus [said] 'do this in remembrance of me'. For whenever you eat this bread and drink this cup, you proclaim the Lord's death until he comes."
>
> *1 Corinthians 11:25–26*

B Decide which of the quotations above could be used to support each statement. Each quotation should only be used once. One has been done for you.

Statement about Holy Communion	Quotation to support this
Holy Communion helps Christians to remember that it is through the death of Jesus that they are able to have eternal life.	
Some Christians believe that through taking the bread and wine, Jesus becomes spiritually present within them. This will help them to follow the example of Jesus in their own lives so that they can truly be his disciple.	
Many Christians perform Holy Communion because Jesus said this was how he should be remembered. They obey Jesus by reciting the same words and performing the same actions that he did during the Last Supper.	*E*
Christians believe the bread and wine represent the blood and body of Jesus. Therefore Holy Communion celebrates and remembers the sacrifice of Jesus and his resurrection.	
Christians believe that by taking Holy Communion they feel part of the same community. They feel closer to one another and are members of one church.	

C How might Holy Communion help a Christian to cope better with difficulties in their own life?

_____

_____

_____

_____

Activity 2.5: Celebrating Holy Communion

  pages 44–45

Three features of Holy Communion are given below. Describe how these are similar within the Orthodox, Catholic, Anglican and Nonconformist Churches, as well as how they are different.

TIP

Do the bread and wine turn into the body and blood of Christ, or do they represent the body and blood of Christ?

Feature	Similarities	Differences
Where the bread and wine are prepared and blessed		
How the bread and wine are shared		
How the bread and wine are viewed or understood		

Exam practice

Use your answers to the previous two activities to help answer this exam question.

Explain **two** ways in which Christians celebrate Holy Communion.   **[5 marks]**

Refer to sacred writings or another source of religious belief and teaching in your answer.

_____

_____

_____

_____

_____

_____

_____

_____

_____

_____

_____

_____

_____

Activity 2.6: Reasons for pilgrimage

S B   pages 46–47

A The following reasons have been given for why a Christian could go on a pilgrimage. Put a tick (✔) or a cross (✘) in the box depending on whether you think each one is a likely or unlikely reason for why a Christian would go on a pilgrimage.

They want to give thanks to God and get closer to him. ☐

They want to go on a holiday. ☐

They want to find a cure for their illness. ☐

They want to show their devotion to God. ☐

They need a break from work and their family. ☐

They want to be cleansed from sin. ☐

They want to renew their faith. ☐

They want to experience the culture of a different country. ☐

B Give **one** more reason for why a Christian might go on a pilgrimage that has not been included in the list above.

_____

_____

Activity 2.7: Pilgrimage to Lourdes and Iona

 page 47

A You have been asked to recommend a pilgrimage site for Christians to visit. Read through the requests below and decide whether you would recommend a pilgrimage to Lourdes or Iona. Explain your choice for each one.

Request: 'I want to strengthen my faith. I want to feel close to God, in a quiet place where I can escape from my busy life.'

Recommendation: _____

Why? _____

_____

Request: 'I want to spend time getting closer to God and to strengthen my faith. I also want to be cured from my illness.'

Recommendation: _____

Why? _____

_____

Request: 'I want to get closer to God and his faithful servant Mary. I want to experience a place where miracles occur.'

Recommendation: _____

Why? _____

_____

B Describe one difference and one similarity between a pilgrimage to Iona and Lourdes.

One similarity might be: _____

_____

One difference might be: _____

_____

Exam practice

Now answer the following exam question.

Which **one** of the following is a popular Christian pilgrimage site? **[1 mark]**

Put a tick (✔) next to the correct answer.

A Lourdes ☐

B Barcelona ☐

C London ☐

D Paris ☐

Activity 2.8: Celebrating Christmas pages 48–49

A The table below describes some of the activities that are often part of Christmas celebrations. Explain the meaning of each activity for Christians. One has been done for you as an example.

Activity	What is the meaning? What does this represent or symbolise?
Decorating houses and streets with lights	*This helps Christians to remember that Jesus came as a light to the world after it had been in darkness since Adam and Eve. He came to show people how they could be reconciled with God.*
Re-enacting or watching nativity scenes	
Attending carol services, which include singing carols and hearing passages from the Bible	
Exchanging cards and gifts	

B The statements below give two reasons why Christmas is still important to Christians today in Great Britain.

For each reason, choose an activity from the table above which links to this reason.

Then explain why you have chosen this activity. How does it support the reason given?

'To me the most important thing about Christmas today is that it reminds me that I must give to the poor. Jesus was poor and there are many people today who are as poor as he was.'	'The most important aspect of Christmas for me is that it is a reminder that God sent his son to save us all. This was a loving gift that was for the benefit of all humans no matter who you are.'
Activity:	**Activity:**

How this activity links to the reason:

_____

_____

_____

_____

_____

How this activity links to the reason:

_____

_____

_____

_____

_____

Activity 2.9: Celebrating Easter

 page 49

Easter is connected to the events surrounding the last week of Jesus' life, but especially:

- the crucifixion and death of Jesus on Good Friday
- the resurrection of Jesus on Easter Sunday.

Complete the table below to show what activities occur during Easter that are connected to these two events.

Event	Activity
The crucifixion and death of Jesus	
The resurrection of Jesus	

Activity 2.10: The significance of Easter

 page 49

A Most Christians consider Easter to be the most important festival. Read the following list of possible reasons for this.

1. It is not as commercialised as Christmas (i.e. it is not used by shops and businesses to make a profit in the same way as Christmas).

2. It reminds Christians that they will survive death.

3. The story of Jesus' death and resurrection is described in all four gospels (the story of Jesus' birth only appears in two gospels).

4. It reminds Christians that their sins are forgiven (both original sin and their individual sins).

5. It shows that Jesus truly was the Son of God as he was resurrected after his crucifixion.

6. It is a more formal occasion and anything that is more solemn must be more important.

B If you had to select **two** of these reasons to explain why Easter is the most important festival for Christians, which **two** would you select and why? Write your ideas below.

The first one I would select would be number: _____

This is because: _____

_____

_____

The second one I would select would be number: _____

This is because: _____

_____

_____

Activity 2.11: Comparing Christmas and Easter

 pages 48–49

Use the table below to show which of these words are only associated with Christmas, which are only associated with Easter, and which apply to both. One has been done for you.

trees	Paschal candle	darkness	Bible readings	cross
lights	eggs	nativity scenes	celebration	carols

Christmas only	Easter only	Both
		Bible readings

Exam practice

Now answer the following exam question.

Explain **two** contrasting examples of how Easter is celebrated in Christianity.

[4 marks]

_____

_____

_____

_____

_____

_____

_____

_____

_____

_____

Activity 2.12: The role of the Church in the local community

pages 50–53

A Here are three arguments for and three arguments against the statement, 'In order to truly follow the example of Jesus, Christians should support food banks'. In the table below, put a tick (✔) next to the arguments that support the statement. Then put a cross (✘) next to the arguments that oppose the statement.

Argument 1

In the Parable of the Sheep and the Goats, Jesus makes it clear that to gain salvation in heaven a Christian must give the hungry and thirsty something to eat and something to drink. Supporting food banks is one way in which a Christian can ensure that the needs of the hungry and thirsty are met because they provide food for such people.

Argument 2

Jesus did not specify how a Christian should show love to a person who is in need, just that they must do this. There are many ways that a Christian can help those in need in the local community, including being a street pastor, donating to food banks, working for a charity, or running a parent and baby group in the local church. Thus it does not matter how a Christian helps as long as they do help.

Argument 3

Being a street pastor could be a better way of following the example of Jesus because this involves true effort on the part of a Christian. This is because they have to give up their time to help vulnerable people in practical ways, such as patrolling the streets to stop antisocial behaviour or helping drunk people get home safely. Just donating food does not show true effort, nor does it really affect your time.

Argument 4

Supporting food banks is a good way of following the example of Jesus as it is something that any Christian can do no matter how busy they are in their day to day lives. All they need to do is donate non-perishable food which is in date to a food bank. There are so many food banks around the country that it would be easy to locate one near to where you live in order to donate food.

Argument 5

In the Parable of the Sheep and the Goats, Jesus makes it clear that salvation is also gained through looking after the sick and visiting people in prison, not just through feeding the hungry in the local community. Therefore, to truly follow the example of Jesus, a Christian could become a prison chaplain or work in medical care.

Argument 6

The way in which Christians follow the example of Jesus should be based on what the specific needs are in their local community. In the UK it is the case that poverty and the need for food is rising. Christians should support food banks because it is what is needed in the UK.

B Choose **one** argument that you find most persuasive. Explain why.

C Choose **one** argument that you think a Christian would find most persuasive. Explain your choice.

TIP

Even if you do not agree with the argument, try to consider which arguments would be most persuasive to a Christian.

D Choose **one** argument that you find to be the weakest argument. Explain why you are not convinced by this argument.

E After evaluating these arguments, write a brief paragraph about whether you agree or disagree with the statement 'In order to truly follow the example of Jesus, Christians should support food banks'.

Key terms

 pages 54–55

A The following key terms are linked to Church growth. Draw lines to connect them to their correct definitions.

Evangelism	Jesus' specific instruction to spread his message to all nations of the world.
Mission	Spreading the message of Christianity through publicly preaching it or through personal witness.
The Great Commission	A person who is sent on a mission to spread Christianity. Normally they will travel to another country for this.
Missionary	The calling of a person or institution to go out into the world and spread the message of Christianity.

B Explain how the following examples link to the key terms given above.

Example	How does this link to mission/The Great Commission/evangelism/missionaries?
The Billy Graham Evangelist Association UK has a project called My Hope. This provides a set of videos where individuals discuss their conversion to Christianity, explaining what their life was like before and how it changed after they became a Christian. They also have an internet evangelism programme where individuals can contact the organisation to learn about others who have converted to Christianity.	_____ _____ _____ _____ _____ _____
TEAM or The Evangelical Alliance Mission is an organisation that helps to send Christians to different parts of the world. They have over 550 Christians in more than 35 countries. They share the message of Jesus as well as serving the local community through healthcare, social justice, community development and tree planting. They aim to send Christians to countries where there is the greatest need for the gospel of Jesus.	_____ _____ _____ _____ _____ _____

Activity 2.13: Church growth

pages 56–57

Answer the following questions about the growth of the Church.

1. Roughly how many Christians are there in the world today?

_____

2. Name **two** continents where Christianity is growing.

_____

3. The number of Christians is falling in Europe and the USA. Give **two** ways that individual Christians or churches in the UK could try to prevent these numbers from continuing to fall.

_____

_____

_____

_____

_____

4. Two quotations from the Bible are given below. Explain what each one tells Christians about how to take part in the Great Commission.

> **❝**Always be prepared to give an answer to everyone who asks you to give the reason for the hope that you have. But do this with gentleness and respect.**❞**
>
> *1 Peter* 3:15

_____

_____

_____

_____

_____

> **❝**Neither do people light a lamp and put it under a bowl. Instead they put it on its stand, and it gives light to everyone in the house. In the same way, let your light shine before others, that they may see your good deeds and glorify your Father in heaven.**❞**
>
> *Matthew* 5:15–16

_____

_____

_____

_____

_____

Exam practice

Use your answers to the previous two activities to help you answer this exam question.

'All Christians should evangelise.'

Evaluate this statement.

In your answer you should:

- refer to Christian teaching
- give reasoned arguments to support this statement
- give reasoned arguments to support a different point of view
- reach a justified conclusion.

[12 marks]

TIP

Make sure that your answer includes clear references to religion, linking to the statement. This can include beliefs, teachings and references to sources of wisdom and authority.

_____

_____

_____

_____

_____

_____

_____

_____

_____

_____

_____

_____

_____

_____

_____

_____

_____

_____

_____

_____

_____

_____

_____

Challenge activity 2.14: Reconciliation

 pages 58–59

Below are four understandings of reconciliation from the staff at Coventry Cathedral, which has a specific focus on trying to bring about reconciliation.

> ❝[Reconciliation is] the transformation of violent or destructive conflict into non-violent and creative disagreement.❞
>
> *Justin Welby (Archbishop of Canterbury)*

> ❝Healing broken relationships [involves] taking the risk of doing precisely what Jesus did and asked his disciples to do.❞
>
> *Reverend Canon Paul Oestreicher*

> ❝It is not about resolving conflict but it's about transforming it […] it isn't about [removing] differences, it's about learning to live and inhabit these differences in a more constructive way.❞
>
> *Canon David Porter*

> ❝It's about the hope that we can live as the people God wants us to be, people who are reconciled with each other and reconciled with him […] it is a journey.❞
>
> *Dr Reverend Canon Sarah Hills*

A The quotations above suggest that reconciliation does not involve removing all conflict but transforming and healing this conflict. What do you think this means?

_____

_____

_____

_____

_____

_____

B Below are photos of two features found at Coventry Cathedral. Choose the one that you think best captures the idea of reconciliation, giving reasons for your answer.

1. A statue of a man and woman embracing

2. A cross with the words 'Father forgive' behind it

The photo that best captures the idea of reconciliation is:

_____

I have chosen this photo because:

_____

_____

_____

C Coventry Cathedral tries to transform and heal conflict in the three main ways described below. Read through these and explain how they could lead to transforming and healing conflict.

Examples	How this could transform and heal conflict
During the Second World War, Coventry Cathedral was bombed. Today the ruins of the old cathedral remain as a memorial and an educational site, acting as a reminder of the destruction that violent conflict can bring and why reconciliation is needed. For example, there are statues in the ruins showing what is involved in reconciliation.	
The Community of the Cross of Nails helps to support any organisation or school which works for peace in one of three areas: 1) healing the wounds of history, 2) learning to live with difference or celebrate diversity, and 3) building a culture for peace. Each centre has a 'cross of nails' plaque displayed and shares the work they are undertaking.	
Saint Michael's House is a specialised centre which trains people in the skills of peacemaking and reconciliation, and provides resources that can be used by those who are seeking to work in this area. It also offers a safe environment for those who are involved in conflict to meet together to try to find a resolution.	

Exam practice

Now answer the following exam question.

Give **two** ways in which Christians can create reconciliation.   **[2 marks]**

1 _____

_____

2 _____

_____

Activity 2.15: Christian persecution

⟨SB⟩ **pages 59–61**

Ⓐ Tick the boxes to indicate whether the following statements about persecution are true or false.

	True	False
Persecution is when someone receives hostility or ill treatment, often due to their race, religion or political beliefs.	☐	☐
The persecution of Christians is a very recent occurrence.	☐	☐
Jesus and the apostle Paul said that Christians should expect to be persecuted.	☐	☐
Some of the places where Christians face serious persecution include North Korea, Canada and Iraq.	☐	☐
Christians do not suffer as much persecution as other faiths.	☐	☐
Christians believe that when they respond to persecution they should try to show love to the person who is persecuting them.	☐	☐
When a Christian is persecuted they can feel as if they are participating in the suffering of Jesus. This can help them through their persecution.	☐	☐

Ⓑ For the statements you have marked as 'false', write one or two sentences with the correct information.

_____

_____

_____

_____

Activity 2.16: Answering a 4-mark exam question

⟨SB⟩ **pages 60–61**

A student has written an answer to the exam question:

'Explain **two** contrasting ways in which Christians might respond to persecution.'

Complete this answer by adding a different point which is developed.

Some Christians might directly support others who are being persecuted. For example, Brother Andrew, Daniel Scalf and David Hathaway smuggled Bibles into Russia to help strengthen the faith of the Christians who were being persecuted there.

_____

_____

_____

_____

_____

Activity 2.17: The Church's response to world poverty   pages 62–63

Complete the tables below to create fact files about two of the following charities:
- CAFOD
- Christian Aid
- Tearfund

TIP

You should know about one of these charities for your exam (it doesn't matter which one). However, it may be useful to know about two of them to help answer a 12-mark question.

Name of the charity	
Short summary of what it does	
Two examples of projects it has carried out	
A source of religious belief and teaching that supports its work	

Name of the charity	
Short summary of what it does	
Two examples of projects it has carried out	
A source of religious belief and teaching that supports its work	

Key Terms Glossary

As you progress through the course, you can collect the meanings of useful terms in the glossary below. You can then use the completed glossaries to revise from.

To do well in the exam you will need to understand these terms and include them in your answers. Tick the shaded circles to record how confident you feel. Use the extra boxes at the end to record any other terms that you have found difficult, along with their definitions.

○ **I recognise this term**

◔ **I understand what this term means**

● **I can use this term in a sentence**

Christmas

Baptism

Easter

Believers' baptism

Evangelism

Bible

Festival

CAFOD

Food bank

Christian Aid

Holy Communion/Eucharist

Infant baptism

Lourdes

Informal prayer

Mission

Informal worship

Non-liturgical worship

Iona

Persecution

Liturgical worship

Pilgrimage

Lord's Prayer

Prayer

Private worship

_____
_____
_____
_____
_____

Worship

_____
_____
_____
_____
_____

Reconciliation

_____
_____
_____
_____
_____

_____
_____
_____
_____
_____

Sacraments

_____
_____
_____
_____
_____

_____
_____
_____
_____
_____

Set prayer

_____
_____
_____
_____
_____

_____
_____
_____
_____
_____

Street pastor

_____
_____
_____
_____
_____

_____
_____
_____
_____
_____

Tearfund

_____
_____
_____
_____

_____
_____
_____
_____

Chapter 3: **Christianity: Exam practice**

Test the 1-mark question

Example

1 | Which **one** of the following describes the belief that God is all powerful? **[1 mark]**

Put a tick (✔) in the box next to the correct answer.

A Omnipresent ☐

B Just ☐

C Incarnation ☐

D Omnipotent ✔ ✔ *(1)*

WHAT WILL THE QUESTION LOOK LIKE?

The 1-mark question will always be a **multiple-choice question** with four answers to choose from. Only one answer is correct. The question will usually start with the words **'Which one of the following…'**.

HOW IS IT MARKED?

You will receive 1 mark for choosing the correct answer by putting a tick in the box next to this answer. You do not need to explain your choice and you must not select more than one answer.

(!) REMEMBER…

Read the question and all of the options **carefully** before selecting your answer. The main reason why marks are lost for this question is because this has not been done.

Many of the 1-mark questions will test you on the meaning of religious terms from the specification, so try to learn all of these words.

Activity

2 | Which **one** of the following describes the execution and death of Jesus? **[1 mark]**

Put a (✔) in the box next to the correct answer.

A Resurrection ☐

B Crucifixion ☐

C Ascension ☐

D Trinity ☐

TIP

Have you completed your glossary of key terms at the ends of Chapters 1 and 2? Learning the meanings of these terms will really help you when answering these questions.

3 | Which **one** of the following is a festival in Christianity?

Put a (✔) in the box next to the correct answer. **[1 mark]**

A Pilgrimage ☐

B Eucharist ☐

C Easter ☐

D Evangelism ☐

Test the 2-mark question

Example

WHAT WILL THE QUESTION LOOK LIKE?

The 2-mark question will always start with the words **'Give two…'** or **'Name two…'**, and a maximum of **2 marks** will be awarded.

1 Name **two** key places of pilgrimage in Christianity. [2 marks]

Lourdes ✓ *(1)*

Iona ✓ *(1)*

HOW IS IT MARKED?

The examiner is looking for two different, correct answers. For each correct response you will receive 1 mark.

(!) **REMEMBER…**

Write your answer on **two separate lines**. This will help you to remember that you need to give **two pieces of information**, each of which should be different.

Keep your answers short. You only need to provide two facts or short ideas; **you don't need to explain them or express any opinions.**

TIP

For 2-mark questions like this one, it is OK to write your answers as single words if that is all that is necessary. You don't need to waste time writing in complete sentences.

Activity

2 Give **two** ways in which a Christian can pray. [2 marks]

The answer below would gain 2 marks. However, most of the information included in the answer is not necessary, as extra detail or development is not required for the 2-mark question. Tick the parts of the answer that would gain a mark, then cross out the parts that would count as development and which are not necessary for this type of question.

Some Christians will say the Lord's Prayer. This is a set prayer that Jesus gave to the disciples so that they would pray in the correct way. Other Christians will say their own prayers which is called informal prayer. They may do this before they eat a meal or go to bed.

TIP

As time is short in the exam, it is important that you do not spend unnecessary time providing extra detail in the lower-marked answers as this will not gain you any additional marks. More time should be spent on the questions that are worth more marks.

3 Name **two** sacraments in Christianity. [2 marks]

1 _____

_____

2 _____

_____

4 Give **two** ways in which a person can gain salvation in Christianity. [2 marks]

1 _____

_____

2 _____

_____

Test the 4-mark question

Example

1 Explain **two** ways in which the belief that God is all loving influences Christians today. **[4 marks]**

One way in which the belief that God is all loving influences Christians today is because it will make them realise that he will forgive their sins. ✓ **(1)**
They may pray to God saying they are truly sorry and asking him to forgive them. ✓ **(1)**

Another way in which this influences Christians is that they will believe that just as God loves them, they should try to love others. ✓ **(1)**
They will try to show this love by helping people in need and showing them compassion. ✓ **(1)**

(!) REMEMBER...

Make **two different points**. Try to show the examiner where each point begins. For example, you could start your answer with 'One way is…' and then move on to your second point by saying 'Another way is…'.

Try to **develop** each point with an example or more explanation.

WHAT WILL THE QUESTION LOOK LIKE?

The 4-mark question will always start with the words **'Explain two…'**, and a maximum of **4 marks** will be awarded.

In the 'Beliefs' section of the exam paper, this question will ask you to explain how a belief or teaching would **influence Christians today**.

In the 'Practices' section of the exam paper, this question will ask you to explain **two contrasting (different) ways** in which a practice is carried out.

HOW IS IT MARKED?

You will be awarded 1 mark for each point and 1 mark for the development of each point. This answer would gain 4 marks because it makes two different points, and both points clearly show extra detail. Both points also show how the belief would influence the ideas and/or actions of a believer.

Activity

2 Explain **two** contrasting reasons why a Christian may go on a pilgrimage. **[4 marks]**

The sample answer below would get 4 marks because there are two contrasting points and each point has extra detail. Add a tick next to each point. Then underline where each point has been developed.

Christians might visit Iona because they believe this place will enable them to get closer to God. This is because it is believed to be a 'thin place' where God is more present than normal.

Some Christians might go to Lourdes because they have an illness. Lourdes is believed to have water which heals people and so they might bathe in the waters to feel better.

3 Explain **two** ways in which the belief in judgement influences Christians today. **[4 marks]**

The sample answer below would get 2 marks for giving two different influences. Develop each influence by giving an example or adding explanation to gain 2 more marks.

This belief means that Christians will make sure they follow God's commandments to do the right thing. ✓ **(1)**

_____

_____

_____

_____

TIP

Remember that for the 4-mark question, in the 'Practices' section, 'contrasting' just means 'different', so you simply need to make two different points in your answer.

Christians believe at the end of time they will answer for what they have done. ✓ **(1)**

_____

_____

_____

_____

4 | Explain **two** ways in which the belief in original sin influences Christians today. **[4 marks]**

_____

_____

_____

_____

_____

_____

_____

_____

_____

_____

> **TIP**
>
> For 'influence' questions like this one, think about how a belief could influence the actions or worldview of an individual believer or community of believers.

5 | Explain **two** contrasting understandings of baptism in Christianity. **[4 marks]**

_____

_____

_____

_____

_____

_____

_____

_____

_____

_____

Test the 5-mark question

Example

1   Explain **two** ways in which Christians celebrate Easter.

Refer to sacred writings or another source of Christian belief and teaching in your answer.   **[5 marks]**

Some Christians will go on a procession in the streets on Good Friday. ✓ **(1)** *They will walk behind someone carrying a wooden cross as it remembers the crucifixion of Jesus.* ✓ **(1)**

Orthodox Christians enter a darkened church at midnight on Easter Saturday. ✓ **(1)** *They take candles with them to symbolise that Jesus rose from the dead.* ✓ **(1)** *They sing hymns to show this with words like "Christ is risen from the dead, trampling down death by death."* ✓ **(1)**

WHAT WILL THE QUESTION LOOK LIKE?

The 5-mark question will always start with the words **'Explain two…'**, and end with **'Refer to sacred writings or another source of Christian belief and teaching in your answer.'** A maximum of 5 marks will be awarded.

HOW IS IT MARKED?

This answer would gain 5 marks. It makes two different points and both points are clearly developed, gaining 4 marks. There is also a reference to a relevant source of Christian belief and teaching, which gains 1 more mark.

ⓘ REMEMBER...

The 5-mark question is similar to the 4-mark question, so try to make **two different points** and **develop** each of them.

The additional instruction in the question asks you to **'refer to sacred writings or another source of Christian belief and teaching'**. Try to think of a reference to the Bible, another religious text like the Nicene Creed, the words of a prayer, or a quotation from the Pope or another Christian leader. You only need one reference.

Activity

2   Explain **two** Christian teachings about the Trinity.

Refer to sacred writings or another source of Christian belief and teaching in your answer.   **[5 marks]**

The sample answer below would get 5 marks because there are two carefully developed points and a reference to a source of Christian belief and teaching. Add a tick next to each point. Then underline where each point has been developed. Finally, circle the reference to sacred writings or another source of Christian belief and teaching.

Christians believe that God is one but he is also three persons. These three persons are God the Father, God the Son and God the Holy Spirit. This can be seen in the Nicene Creed which mentions the Father almighty, the Son of God and the Holy Spirit.

Christians believe that all persons of the Trinity are fully God but they are not the same. Even though they are different they are still equally as important as each other.

3 Explain **two** Christian beliefs about life after death.

Refer to sacred writings or another source of Christian belief and teaching in your answer. **[5 marks]**

The sample answer below would get 4 marks because there are two developed points. However, the student has not supported these with a reference to sacred writings or another source of Christian belief and teaching. Three quotations are given below. Select one of these and use it to extend one of the points below so that the answer can gain the full 5 marks.

Christians believe that when they die they will be judged according to the actions they performed on earth. To go to heaven, they need to have followed the teachings and actions of Jesus.

_____

_____

_____

In Christianity it is believed that after death some people will go to hell. This is a place that is full of fire, pain and torment where there is no God.

_____

_____

_____

> **❝**The angels will come out and separate the wicked from the righteous and throw them into the blazing furnace, where there will be weeping and gnashing of teeth. **❞**
>
> *Matthew 13:49–50*

> **❝**For God so loved the world that he gave his one and only Son. **❞**
>
> *John 3:16*

> **❝**All the nations will be gathered before him, and he will separate the people one from another as a shepherd separates the sheep from the goats. **❞**
>
> *Matthew 25:32*

TIP

For the 5-mark question it is important that your reference to sacred writings or another source of Christian belief and teaching is relevant to the question. Always think carefully about whether your choice helps to support the point you are making.

4 Explain **two** ways in which Christians use the Bible.

Refer to sacred writings or another source of Christian belief and teaching in your answer. **[5 marks]**

Four sentence starters are given below. Use **two** of these to write a complete answer to this question. You will need to develop both of these points and also refer to sacred writings or another source of Christian belief and teaching to gain full marks.

Christians listen to Bible readings during Holy Communion...

Christians may use the Bible during private worship...

Passages from the Bible are said during baptism...

Missionaries will use the Bible...

_____

_____

_____

_____

_____

_____

_____

_____

_____

_____

> ## TIP
> You don't need to quote a source of religious belief and teaching word-for-word, but try to say where it came from. For example, whether it came from the Bible, a document produced by the Church, a speech by the Pope, etc.

5 | Explain **two** Christian beliefs about Jesus' resurrection.

Refer to sacred writings or another source of Christian belief and teaching in your answer.   **[5 marks]**

_____

_____

_____

_____

_____

_____

_____

_____

_____

_____

_____

6 | Explain **two** ways in which prayer is significant to Christians.

Refer to sacred writings or another source of Christian belief and teaching in your answer.   **[5 marks]**

_____

_____

_____

_____

_____

_____

_____

_____

_____

_____

_____

Test the 12-mark question

Example

1 'Jesus is the best way to understand God.'

Evaluate this statement.

In your answer you should:

- refer to Christian teaching
- give reasoned arguments to support this statement
- give reasoned arguments to support a different point of view
- reach a justified conclusion. **[12 marks]**

[SPaG 3 marks]

WHAT WILL THE QUESTION LOOK LIKE?

The 12-mark question will always ask you to **evaluate** a statement. The bullet points underneath the statement will tell you the things the examiner expects to see in your answer. Here, it says you need to 'refer to Christian teachings', so make sure you write about core Christian beliefs and include important sources of religious belief and teaching. You also need to give reasoned arguments to support two different points of view. The final bullet point will always ask you to 'reach a justified conclusion'.

HOW IS IT MARKED?

The examiner will mark your answer using a mark scheme based on level descriptors, similar to the one opposite.

In the 'Beliefs' section of the exam paper, you will also be assessed on the quality of your written communication in the 12-mark question. A maximum of 3 marks will be awarded for accurate **spelling, punctuation and grammar** as well as the use of a range of **specialist terms**. Allow yourself time in the exam to check that you have done this in your answer.

! REMEMBER...

To evaluate the statement, you need to have:

- A paragraph or paragraphs in support of the statement which explain why some people might agree with the statement, and give reasons (including Christian views) to support this.
- A paragraph or paragraphs opposing the statement which explain why other people might disagree with the statement and give reasons (including Christian views) to support this view.
- A justified conclusion which explains which side of the argument you think has the strongest evidence, briefly referring to the evidence as you write. You should explain why you think this is the strongest evidence/argument in support or in opposition of the statement.

What might make a strong argument?

- Based on a religious teaching/source of authority
- Based on scientific evidence
- The majority of Christians accept it

What might make a weak argument?

- Based on personal opinion rather than religious teaching
- A popular idea that has no scientific basis
- Very few Christians would agree with it

Level descriptors

Level 4 (10–12 marks)	• A well-argued response, reasoned consideration of different points of view. • Logical chains of reasoning leading to judgement(s) supported by knowledge and understanding of relevant evidence and information. • **References to religion applied to the issue.**
Level 3 (7–9 marks)	• Reasoned consideration of different points of view. • Logical chains of reasoning that draw on knowledge and understanding of relevant evidence and information. • **Clear reference to religion.**
Level 2 (4–6 marks)	• Reasoned consideration of a point of view. • A logical chain of reasoning drawing on knowledge and understanding of relevant evidence and information. OR • Recognition of different points of view, each supported by relevant reasons/evidence. • **Maximum of Level 2 if there is no reference to religion.**
Level 1 (1–3 marks)	• Point of view with reason(s) stated in support.

Here are four sample answers to the example question on the opposite page. Each answer would be awarded a different Level. Read through the answers to get an idea of what a Level 1, 2, 3 or 4 answer looks like.

Level 1 sample answer

This is a Level 1 answer because:

- it only gives a point of view for one side of the argument
- it only gives a basic reason for this point of view which is not developed
- it shows a very limited understanding of Christianity
- there is no conclusion.

To improve this answer the student should:

- develop the point of view they have stated
- include more teachings from Christianity
- include a developed point of view for the other side of the argument
- reach a justified conclusion explaining whether the argument is strong or weak.

This is true because this is the main reason why Jesus is here. It makes sense if you think about it because it is what Jesus is here for. Jesus helps people know God as he is God. He just would not be here if this was not true.

TIP

'Jesus helps people know God as he is God' is a good point but it is not developed. The student also needs to give arguments that support another point of view.

Level 2 sample answer

This is a Level 2 answer because:

- it refers to different arguments for and against the statement, which have some development
- it refers to some teachings in Christianity
- it comes to a conclusion about which side is correct.

To improve this answer the student could:

- develop the different arguments linked to the statement with relevant evidence
- include more reference to relevant teachings within Christianity
- develop the conclusion to explain why one argument is stronger than the other.

This statement is true because Jesus is supposed to be God on earth. He tells people what God is like as he is God. But it is also not true because there are other ways of knowing God such as through the Holy Spirit. A person can learn about God there because the Holy Spirit is God too. In conclusion I disagree with the statement as the Spirit also tells you about God.

TIP
This student has given a conclusion providing a reason why they disagree with the statement. But this needs to be further developed to become fully justified.

Level 3 sample answer

This is a Level 3 answer because:

- it has developed and relevant arguments for and against the statement
- it refers to relevant Christian teachings
- it comes to a brief, reasoned consideration of the points of view in the conclusion.

To improve this answer the student could:

- provide more relevant development or detail in their arguments for and against the statement
- include more detailed reference to relevant teachings within Christianity
- give a more justified conclusion where all of the elements presented in the answer are judged.

In this essay I am going to discuss why some people agree that Jesus is the best way to know God and why some people disagree with this.

Most Christians will agree with this statement that Jesus is the best way to know about God. They would agree because Jesus is said to be God in a human body. They believe Jesus shows them things about God such as he is loving and this means they can know what he is like. Knowing that God is loving is really important as Christians believe this is true.

However, some Christians disagree with this statement and do not believe this is the best way to know God. They believe there are other good ways to know God such as through his creation. For example, you could look to this world to find something out about God. Muslims would also disagree because they do not believe Jesus is part of God.

In conclusion, I disagree with this statement because there are other important ways to know God such as in creation.

TIP
You don't need to include an introduction in your answer to a 12-mark question. Instead just go straight into the arguments for and against the statement.

TIP
It is a good idea to start a new paragraph when you give a different point of view.

TIP
You should not include reference to other religious worldviews in the Christianity exam paper. This will not gain you any marks and because it is irrelevant, it could even prevent you from gaining the highest marks.

Level 4 sample answer

This is a Level 4 answer because:

- there are developed reasons for and against the statement which are fully relevant
- there is accurate and detailed reference to relevant teachings within Christianity
- it is clear the student knows a lot about the topic, and the whole answer is clearly linked to the statement
- there is a justified conclusion which makes a judgement about which side is stronger based on relevant evidence and information.

TIP

This is a very well-structured response with a clear line of reasoning that leads to a justified conclusion. It is worth spending a bit of time planning your own response. Start by thinking of arguments for and against the statement. Think of evidence you could use to support this. Remember to end with a justified conclusion, stating which side you find more convincing and explain why you think this.

Some Christians believe that it is only through Jesus that a person can truly know God. The main reason for this is because they believe the Bible says Jesus is the incarnation of God. For example, John's Gospel says Jesus is the 'Word' who was present at creation and the other gospels says he is the 'Son of God'. This point can be strengthened by the Christian belief that Jesus also shows people what God is like and how he wants them to live. For example, Jesus shows that God is all loving and that he wants people to show love to one's neighbour. Jesus also makes it clear that it is through him that people know God as he said: 'I am the way and the truth and the life. No one comes to the Father except through me.' Therefore, it is true that Jesus is the main way for a Christian to find out about God because he is God incarnate who deliberately came to earth to teach people who he was and how they should live.

TIP

Remember that for the 12-mark question in the 'Beliefs' section of the exam paper you will be awarded an extra 3 marks for SPaG. This student would gain the full 3 marks because their spelling, punctuation and grammar are accurate and they have also used a range of specialist terms (such as 'incarnation' and 'Trinity').

However, most Christians would also disagree with this statement. They would argue that although it is true that Jesus is God incarnate, this does not mean he is the best way to know about God. The main reason why they would argue this is because the Bible and Apostles' Creed shows that Jesus is only one part of the Trinity and that all three parts are needed to understand God, not just one. The other parts are the Holy Spirit and God the Father. For example, through God the Father Christians can learn that God is all powerful as he created the world just by speaking. Therefore, although it is true that Christians can learn a lot about God through Jesus, it is not true that this is the best way for Christians to know God, as the other parts of the Trinity should also be looked at as well in order to know God as only then will you get a complete picture.

TIP

Try to use accurate and relevant sources of religious belief and teaching to support the points you are making.

In conclusion I do not agree with this statement. This is because although I think Christians do believe they will learn a lot about God through Jesus, I think they will also agree that they need to look at all three parts of the Trinity to truly know God. This is seen in the Apostles, Creed as well as the Bible. Therefore, it is not Jesus alone that will help them to know God but also the Father and the Holy Spirit, as all are part of the Trinity.

TIP

The student has written a justified conclusion, expressing a judgement and giving reasons for why they have reached that judgement.

Activity

2 'Following the Law by performing good deeds and serving others will lead to salvation.'

Evaluate this statement.

In your answer you should:

- refer to Christian teaching
- give reasoned arguments to support this statement
- give reasoned arguments to support a different point of view
- reach a justified conclusion.

[12 marks]
[SPaG 3 marks]

A Read the sample answer below.

The belief that following the Law by serving other people and performing good deeds will lead to salvation is known as salvation through good works. The main or most convincing reason why Christians would agree with this is because there are passages in the Bible, one of the highest sources of authority in Christianity, which show that salvation can occur through good works. For example, this is seen in the Parable of the Sheep and the Goats, where Jesus said the sheep would go to heaven because they had given food, water, clothing and hospitality to those who were poor or in need, whereas the goats would go to hell as they had not done this. Therefore, as this passage clearly shows salvation is based on good deeds, it is true that following the Law will lead to salvation.

However, some Christians would disagree that salvation is gained through following the Law alone as the Bible also shows that salvation by grace is also needed. Salvation by grace is when God helps a person to be saved because they have faith in Jesus. For example, Christians must also believe Jesus is the incarnation of God and have faith in him, as only then will God help them go to heaven. Therefore, these Christians would argue that salvation is only gained if a Christian follows both the Law and has faith in Jesus, as only then will God save them.

After considering both sides of the argument, I think it is both true and not true that following the Law will lead to salvation. I think it is true because the Bible says that following the Law by performing good works will lead to salvation (as seen in the Parable of the Sheep and the Goats), but I also think it is not true because the Bible also says that grace is needed to gain salvation, which means a person has to have faith in Jesus as well. Therefore, although it is convincing to say that in Christianity following the Law is needed for salvation, it is only fully convincing if this also includes the need to have faith in Jesus or the grace of God as well.

B Now answer the following questions about the sample answer above.

1. The student makes one main argument to support the statement. What is it?

_____

_____

_____

_____

2. How do they develop this point?

_____

_____

_____

_____

_____

3. The student makes one main argument against the statement. What is it?

_____

_____

_____

_____

4. How do they develop this point?

_____

_____

_____

_____

_____

5. The question says you should 'refer to Christian teaching'. Using a coloured pen, highlight any references to Christian teaching that you can find.

6. The student uses a range of specialist terms, which is necessary for gaining 3 SPaG marks. Write examples of these terms below.

_____

_____

_____

_____

7. The question asks you to 'reach a justified conclusion'. Circle the sentence where the student gives their judgement. Then underline the sentence where they summarise their evidence.

3 | 'Worship in Christianity should be liturgical.'

Evaluate this statement.

In your answer you should:

- refer to Christian teaching

- give reasoned arguments to support this statement

- give reasoned arguments to support a different point of view

- reach a justified conclusion.   **[12 marks]**

Here is the beginning of a response to the question above, which gives some arguments in support of the statement. To complete the answer you need to give developed arguments against the statement and reach a justified conclusion.

Complete the answer below.

- Begin your first paragraph with the sentence, 'However, many Christians would disagree with these ideas because…'

- Include reference to Christian teachings

- Finally, add a justified conclusion. This could begin, 'After considering both sides of the argument, the most convincing position is…'

Some Christians might agree with this statement because liturgical worship follows a set pattern all of the time. Through this a Christian will always know that they have worshipped God in the correct way and have not forgotten anything that is essential. For example, they will know when they have to pray and how and when they need to receive the bread and wine. Liturgical worship often includes a sermon where a Christian will be able to learn about the message of Jesus. This will help them to have a clear understanding of what Jesus said and did as well as how they should live their lives. This could be essential as they evangelise the message of Jesus to others. Therefore, it could be said to be true that worship in Christianity should be liturgical as this will ensure a person worships correctly and also receives a true understanding of the Christian message.

_____

_____

_____

_____

_____

_____

_____

_____

_____

_____

_____

_____

4 'The most important belief about the nature of God is that he is omnipotent.'

Evaluate this statement.

In your answer you should:

- refer to Christian teaching
- give reasoned arguments to support this statement
- give reasoned arguments to support a different point of view
- reach a justified conclusion.

[12 marks]
[SPaG 3 marks]

Read the sample answer below.

This is a Level 2 answer. **Rewrite this so that it gains a Level 3, or if possible, a Level 4.**

To make it a Level 3 answer you need to:

- include developed and relevant arguments for and against the statement
- refer to relevant Christian teachings
- show a brief, reasoned consideration of the points of view in the conclusion.

To make it a Level 4 answer you need to:

- include developed reasons for and against the statement which are fully relevant
- make accurate and detailed reference to relevant teachings within Christianity
- show that you know a lot about the topic, and how the whole answer clearly links to the statement
- justify the conclusion by making a judgement about which side is stronger based on relevant evidence and information.

In this essay I am going to explore the statement that the most important attribute of God is his omnipotence.

Christians would agree with the statement that the most important belief about God is his omnipotence. This is because they would say that God has to be this in order to create the world. Christians would not agree with this statement though as well. They would say his love is more important. I have heard many Christians say this and so it is very popular. In conclusion I think that love is more important that omnipotence.

5 'All Christians should become street pastors.'

Evaluate this statement.

In your answer you should:

- refer to Christian teaching
- give reasoned arguments to support this statement
- give reasoned arguments to support a different point of view
- reach a justified conclusion. **[12 marks]**

> **(!) REMEMBER...**
>
> - Focus your answer on the statement you are asked to evaluate. Do not include irrelevant information, views from other religions or non-religious views.
> - Try to write at least three paragraphs – one with arguments to support the statement, one with arguments to support a different point of view, and a final paragraph with a justified conclusion stating which side you think is more convincing, and why.
> - Make sure you fully develop your points with evidence that includes teachings from Christianity.
> - Include a justified conclusion where you make a judgement about which side is stronger based on the evidence you have discussed. You can use phrases such as 'I think this is a convincing argument because...'

6 'The ascension truly shows Jesus is the Son of God.'

Evaluate this statement.

In your answer you should:

- refer to Christian teaching
- give reasoned arguments to support this statement
- give reasoned arguments to support a different point of view
- reach a justified conclusion.

[12 marks]
[SPaG 3 marks]

_____

_____

_____

_____

_____

_____

_____

_____

_____

_____

_____

_____

_____

_____

_____

_____

_____

_____

_____

_____

_____

Chapter 4: **Buddhism: Beliefs and teachings**

Activity 4.1: Key events in the Buddha's life

pages 8–15

Five key events in the Buddha's life are given or described in the table below. Complete the table by:

- explaining what happened during the Buddha's 'life of luxury' and time spent as an ascetic
- naming the other three events by matching up the terms below to the correct descriptions.

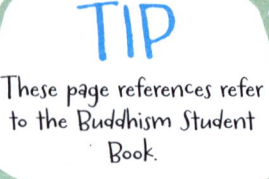

TIP

These page references refer to the Buddhism Student Book.

enlightenment   birth   witnessing the four sights

Event	Description – what happened?
	This is when Siddhartha Gautama entered the world. Some Buddhist sources say that Siddhartha could immediately walk and talk.
Life of luxury	
	This is when Siddhartha first became aware of life's suffering. After escaping the palace, Siddhartha witnessed the pains of illness, old age and death. He was also inspired by a holy man.
Asceticism	
	This is when Siddhartha became 'the Buddha'. Through meditation he became aware of the true nature of reality.

Activity 4.2: Assessing the importance of events in the Buddha's life pages 8–15

Read the following text and then answer the questions below.

Which event in the Buddha's life was the most important? Here the student on the left is arguing that witnessing the four sights was the most important, while the student on the right is giving a reason for why the Buddha's ascetic period was the most important.

> Without experiencing the four sights, Siddhartha may never have been motivated to leave the palace and may never have become the Buddha.

> While Siddhartha was an ascetic, he overcame a lot of temptation and desire using his own determination and will, and this sets a strong moral example for Buddhists today.

1. Give another argument to support the idea that witnessing the four sights was the most important event in the Buddha's life.

_____

_____

_____

_____

2. Now give an argument to support the idea that the Buddha's enlightenment was the most important event in his life.

_____

_____

_____

_____

3. Siddhartha's father didn't want his son to become a holy man, so he sheltered him from the outside world and gave him a life of luxury. Do you think this life of luxury was important in turning Siddhartha into a religious leader? Explain your answer.

_____

_____

_____

_____

4. It was during Siddhartha's time spent living as an ascetic that he discovered the 'middle way'. Why is this discovery so important to Buddhists today?

_____

_____

_____

_____

TIP
Remember that for the 12-mark question, you need to give more than one side to an argument. Try to think about different viewpoints on each topic as you work through this book.

Activity 4.3: The influence of the Buddha's life

 pages 8–15

A Different parts of the Buddha's life influence Buddhists today in a number of ways. Five ways that Buddhists are influenced today are given below. Match up each term given below to the correct influence from Buddha's life.

Birth   Life of luxury   Witnessing the four sights   Ascetism   Enlightenment

Influence	Part of the Buddha's life
It may encourage Buddhists to perform pilgrimage to Lumbini	
It may encourage Buddhists to avoid living a life of denial and self-imposed suffering	
It may encourage Buddhists to attempt to relieve the suffering that is witnessed and experienced in the world	
It may encourage Buddhists to engage in the practice of meditation	
It may encourage Buddhists to avoid a life of extreme sensual and material pleasures	

B Now give another **two** ways that a part of the Buddha's life might influence Buddhists today.

1 _____

_____

2 _____

_____

Exam practice

Use your answers to the previous activities to help you answer this exam question.

Explain **two** ways in which the Buddha's enlightenment influences Buddhists today.   **[4 marks]**

_____

_____

_____

_____

_____

_____

_____

_____

TIP

To develop your points here, you could go into more detail about the actions that Buddhists take because of each influence. For example, if one influence is that Buddhists meditate, you could explain how they meditate.

Activity 4.4: The Dhamma

pages 16–17

Answer the following questions about the Dhamma.

1. The term 'Dhamma' has a number of slightly different meanings. One is that it is the 'truth' about the nature of existence or reality. Give another meaning below.

    _____

    _____

    _____

2. The Buddha wanted his followers to question and test his teachings. Why do you think he wanted this?

    _____

    _____

    _____

    _____

3. The Buddha compared his teachings to a raft that is used to cross a river: the raft is important for crossing the river, but it has to be left behind once you have reached the shore. What do you think the Buddha was trying to teach when he made this comparison?

    _____

    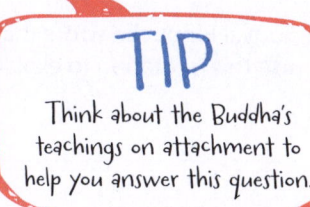

    TIP
    Think about the Buddha's teachings on attachment to help you answer this question.

    _____

    _____

    _____

4. The Dhamma is one of the three refuges in Buddhism. By following the Dhamma, what do you think Buddhists are seeking 'refuge' from?

    _____

    _____

    _____

    _____

5. The Dhamma is important to Buddhists because they believe it reduces suffering and leads them to become more compassionate. Give **two** more reasons why the Dhamma is important to Buddhists.

    _____

    _____

    _____

    _____

Challenge activity 4.5: Dependent arising

pages 18–19

Dependent arising is the idea that:

- everything depends on conditions (nothing is independent)
- everything changes (because everything depends on conditions that are themselves changing).

A An example is given below to illustrate dependent arising. Fill in the rest of the table to show how the examples of a person's job and a broken arm can also illustrate dependent arising.

Example	How does it depend on other conditions?	How does this create a constant process of change?
A tree	It depends on rain and sunshine to survive.	The weather is always changing and this affects how the tree grows and changes with the seasons.
A person's job		
A broken arm		

B Sogyal Rinpoche wrote that 'every wave is related to every other wave'. In your own words, use this quotation to explain what dependent arising means.

_____

_____

_____

_____

C How do you think the idea of dependent arising might affect a Buddhist's attitude towards taking care of the environment? Explain your answer.

_____

_____

_____

_____

D Dependent arising is the idea that everything depends on conditions. Which conditions affect whether a Buddhist is reborn into a good world or a bad world?

_____

_____

_____

_____

Activity 4.6: The three marks of existence

 pages 20–25

The three marks of existence are the three characteristics which are fundamental to all things. Using the terms in the left-hand column below, write an entire paragraph of text to explain one of the three marks of existence. The first mark of existence has been started for you.

Terms	Explanation
dukkha suffering three ordinary change attachment enlightenment	*Dukkha is one of the three marks of existence. This says that there are **three** types of **suffering**.*
anicca impermanence changing attachment	
anatta no fixed self permanent the five aggregates	

Sources of religious belief and teaching

 pages 20–25

Answer the following questions.

1. Which mark of existence does each of the quotations below refer to?

Quotation	Which mark of existence?
"all conditioned things are impermanent" The Buddha in the *Dhammapada*, verse 277	
"all conditioned phenomena are dukkha" The Buddha in the *Dhammapada*, verse 278	
"all phenomena are without self" The Buddha in the *Dhammapada*, verse 279	

2. The story of Kisa Gotami is told in the Dhammapāda. How does this story help Buddhists to understand the concepts of dukkha and anicca?

_____

_____

_____

_____

_____

_____

_____

3. The story of Nagasena and the chariot is told in a Buddhist text called *The Questions of King Milinda*. How does this story help Buddhists to understand the concept of anatta?

_____

_____

_____

_____

_____

_____

TIP

These two stories can be used as 'sources of Buddhist belief and teaching' in your exam. You don't need to learn the stories by heart but it could be useful to be able to give a brief summary of them and to know how they are relevant to Buddhist teachings.

Activity 4.7: How the three marks of existence influence Buddhists today

 pages 20–25

Decide which mark of existence is being referred to in each of the situations below. Then give another way that this mark might influence Buddhists today.

1. This mark may encourage Buddhists to fear death less, as they see it not as an end to the 'self' but as the transition of a person's kammic energy from one body to the next.

Mark: _____

Another way this mark might influence Buddhists today:

_____

_____

_____

2. This mark may encourage Buddhists to try to improve the lives of those living in poverty so they suffer less, for example by volunteering for a charity.

Mark: _____

Another way this mark might influence Buddhists today:

_____

_____

_____

3. This mark may encourage Buddhists to become more resilient to change, by accepting that change is an inevitable part of life.

Mark: _____

Another way this mark might influence Buddhists today:

_____

_____

_____

Exam practice

Now answer the following exam question.

Name **two** marks of existence. **[2 marks]**

1 _____

_____

2 _____

_____

TIP
You do not need to write full sentences to answer this question. For a 2-mark question like this one, one-word answers are fine.

Activity 4.8: The first three noble truths

 pages 26–33

Answer the following questions about the first three noble truths.

1. The first noble truth is that suffering exists. Give **three** types of suffering that everyone experiences according to the Buddha.

1 _____

2 _____

3 _____

2. For Buddhists, how does it help to acknowledge that suffering is an unavoidable part of life?

_____

_____

_____

_____

> **TIP**
>
> In his book *The Four Noble Truths*, the Dalai Lama suggests that the Four Noble Truths are the foundation of Buddhism and the key to understanding the Buddha's Dhamma. You can use this as a source of religious belief and teaching in your exam to show that the Four Noble Truths are essential to Buddhism.

3. The second noble truth is to do with the origins of suffering. Buddhism teaches that one of the main reasons why people suffer is because of 'craving'. What does this mean?

_____

_____

_____

_____

_____

4. The third noble truth is that suffering can be stopped. According to this noble truth, what do Buddhists have to overcome in order to end suffering?

_____

_____

_____

_____

_____

5. If Buddhists are able to overcome suffering then it is possible to achieve enlightenment. Two characteristics of someone who has achieved enlightenment are given below. Add **two** more.

1 *They have achieved a state of complete happiness and peace (nibbana).*

2 *They naturally behave according to the five moral precepts.*

3 _____

4 _____

Activity 4.9: Buddhist attitudes based on the Four Noble Truths **pages 26–35**

Two different viewpoints are given below. For each one, explain how you think a Buddhist might respond.

> Everyone suffers so there's no point in trying to overcome it. You just have to try to live with it.

_____

_____

_____

_____

_____

> I really enjoy going on holiday but I hate when it's over, so maybe it's better not to go on holiday at all.

_____

_____

_____

_____

_____

Activity 4.10: Key ideas associated with the Four Noble Truths **pages 26–35**

Below are some key ideas associated with the Four Noble Truths. For each one, write a number from 1 to 4 in the box to show which truth you think it is associated with. One has been done for you as an example.

The existence of suffering [*1*]	The three poisons [ ]	The end of suffering [ ]
The threefold way [ ]	The causes of suffering [ ]	Craving [ ]
Dukkha [ ]	The Eightfold Path [ ]	The cure for suffering [ ]

Sources of religious belief and teaching

 pages 26–35

A Three quotations about the Four Noble Truths are given below. For each quotation, decide which noble truth it is referring to. Then explain what you think the quotation means.

Quotation	Which noble truth?	What does it mean?
" It is this craving which leads to renewed existence **"** The Buddha in the *Sumyutta Nikaya*, volume 5, p.421		
" The insight is simply […] that there is this suffering without making it personal. **"** Ajahn Sumedho (American Buddhist monk)		
" [This noble truth] is the remainderless fading away and cessation of that same craving. **"** The Buddha in the *Sumyutta Nikaya*, volume 5, p.421		

" But if any one goes to the Buddha, the Doctrine and the Order as a refuge, he perceives with proper knowledge the Four Noble Truths: Suffering, the arising of suffering, and the overcoming of suffering, and the noble eightfold path leading to the cessation of suffering. **"**
The Buddha in the *Dhammapada*, verses 190–191

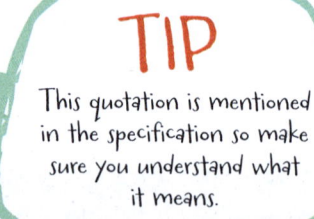

TIP
This quotation is mentioned in the specification so make sure you understand what it means.

B Based on the quotation above, what **three** pieces of advice could you give to someone who wanted to overcome suffering?

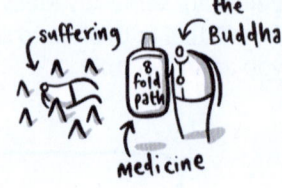

1 _____

_____

_____

2 _____

_____

_____

3 _____

_____

_____

Activity 4.11: Practising the Eightfold Path

 pages 34–35

Six aspects of the Eightfold Path are given below. For each one, give **two** examples of different ways that Buddhists can practise this aspect. One has been done for you as an example.

Aspect of the Eightfold Path	Example of how a Buddhist can practise this
Right effort	1 *Putting effort into meditating before work every day* 2
Right livelihood	1 2
Right speech	1 2
Right intention	1 2
Right action	1 2
Right understanding	1 2

Exam practice

Use your answers to the previous two activities to answer this exam question.

Explain **two** Buddhist teachings about the Eightfold Path.

Refer to sacred writings or another source of Buddhist belief and teaching in your answer.   **[5 marks]**

_____

_____

_____

_____

_____

_____

_____

_____

_____

_____

_____

TIP

Remember that you need to develop your points in your answer to the 5-mark question. A useful way to do this is with the words 'This means that...' or 'For example...'.

Activity 4.12: Different forms of Buddhism

pages 36–39

In each of the boxes below:

- write the letter 'T' if you think the word or phrase applies to Theravada Buddhism
- write the letter 'M' if you think the word or phrase applies to Mahayana Buddhism
- write both 'T' and 'M' if you think the word or phrase applies to both.

One has been done for you as an example.

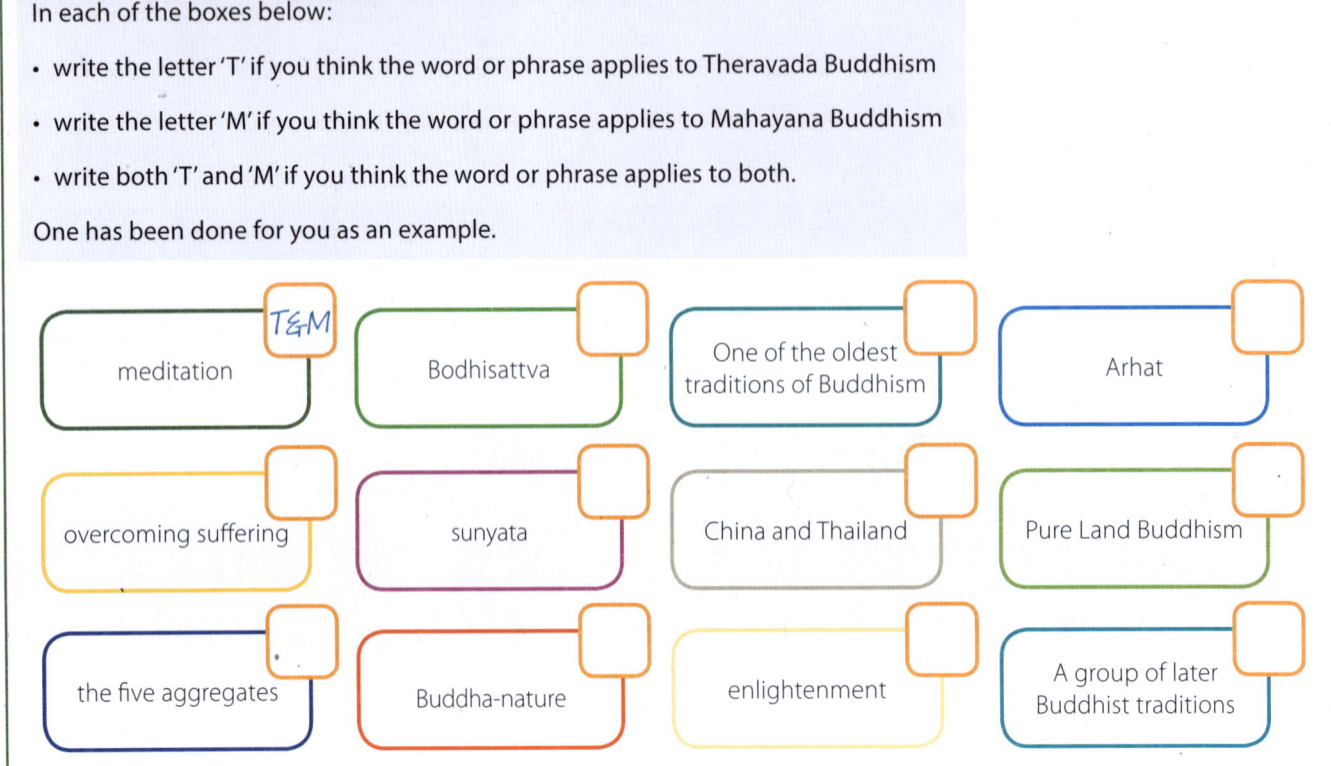

meditation `T&M`

Bodhisattva

One of the oldest traditions of Buddhism

Arhat

overcoming suffering

sunyata

China and Thailand

Pure Land Buddhism

the five aggregates

Buddha-nature

enlightenment

A group of later Buddhist traditions

Activity 4.13: The five aggregates

 pages 36–37

Answer the following questions on the five aggregates.

1. Name each of the five aggregates described in the table below.

Aggregate	Description
	A person's thoughts and opinions about what they are experiencing.
	A person's general awareness of the world around them.
	Recognising or perceiving what things are, based on previous experiences.
	A person's physical body.
	The feelings or sensations that occur when a person comes into contact with things.

2. Explain how the five aggregates link to the concept of anatta.

_____

_____

_____

_____

_____

_____

3. Theravada Buddhism teaches that the five aggregates are continually changing, which means that a person's 'self' is continually changing. Give **one** argument or piece of evidence that could be used to suggest that a person's 'self' is continually changing.

_____

_____

_____

_____

4. Now give **one** argument or piece of evidence that could be used to suggest that a person's 'self' is not continually changing.

_____

_____

_____

_____

Activity 4.14: The human personality in Mahayana Buddhism
[SB] **pages 38–39**

A Tick the correct boxes to show whether the following statements are true or false.

	True	False
Sunyata means 'emptiness'.	☐	☐
Sunyata means that nothing truly exists – everything is an illusion.	☐	☐
Sunyata is very similar to anatta.	☐	☐
Sunyata only applies to humans.	☐	☐
Sunyata helps Buddhists to develop trust and compassion as they realise that everything interlinks with and depends on everything else.	☐	☐
Buddha-nature is the idea that Buddhists who have been ordained have the essence or nature of a Buddha inside them.	☐	☐
A Buddhist reaches Buddhahood when they achieve enlightenment and become a Buddha.	☐	☐

B For the statements you have marked as 'false', write one or two sentences with the correct information.

_____

_____

_____

_____

_____

_____

Exam practice

Now answer the following exam question.

Which **one** of the following is the best description of sunyata? **[1 mark]**

Put a tick (✓) in the box next to the correct answer.

A Humans have a 'soul' or 'self' ☐

B Nothing has a fixed, independent, unchanging nature ☐

C Everyone has the potential to become a Buddha ☐

D Humans' souls transfer to a new body when they die ☐

Key terms

pages 40–41

Five sentences are given below about human destiny in Theravada and Mahayana Buddhism. For each of the sentences below, identify which key term could be used instead of the text written in bold and then write the word or phrase in the box provided.

One has been done for you as an example.

1. Theravada Buddhists aim to become an **enlightened, perfected person**.

Key term	

2. Theravada Buddhists try to do this by **overcoming greed, hatred and ignorance** and putting into practice the **Buddha's teachings**.

Key term 1	
Key term 2	*Eightfold Path*

3. Mahayana Buddhists aim to become a **person who is enlightened**, who stays in the **cycle of life and death**.

Key term 1	
Key term 2	

4. Mahayana Buddhists aim to remain in this world because of **a feeling they should care for others**.

Key term	

5. To try to become enlightened, Mahayana Buddhists focus on **six characteristics which they try to perfect in their lives**.

Key term	

Activity 4.15: Arhats and Bodhisattvas

pages 40–41

Answer these questions on Arhats and Bodhisattvas.

1. A Bodhisattva vow is 'However innumerable sentient beings are; I vow to save them.'
   What does this vow tell you about the role of a Bodhisattva?

   _____

   _____

   _____

   _____

   _____

   _____

   _____

2. Give **one** reason why some Buddhists might consider it easier to become a Bodhisattva than an Arhat.

   _____

   _____

   _____

   _____

   _____

3. Now give **one** reason why some Buddhists might consider it easier to become an Arhat than a Bodhisattva.

   _____

   _____

   _____

   _____

4. Many Tibetan Buddhists consider the Dalai Lama to be an earthly Bodhisattva. How might each of the
   following quotations help to suggest that the Dalai Lama is a Bodhisattva?

   > **“**Generosity is the most natural outward expression of an inner attitude of compassion
   > and loving-kindness. **”**
   >
   > Tenzin Gyatso, 14th Dalai Lama

   _____

   _____

   _____

   _____

> ❝Be kind whenever possible. It is always possible.❞
>
> Tenzin Gyatso, 14th Dalai Lama

_____

_____

_____

> ❝A disciplined mind leads to happiness, and an undisciplined mind leads to suffering.❞
>
> Tenzin Gyatso, 14th Dalai Lama

_____

_____

_____

Activity 4.16: Pure Land Buddhism

S B   pages 42–43

Answer the following questions about Pure Land Buddhism.

1. Which Buddhist tradition does Pure Land Buddhism belong to?

_____

2. Where is Pure Land Buddhism mainly practised today?

_____

3. What is the name of the Buddha worshipped by Pure Land Buddhists?

_____

4. Give **three** of the practices that Pure Land Buddhists are encouraged to follow to be reborn in the pure land.

   1 _____

   2 _____

   3 _____

5. Give **two** reasons why Pure Land Buddhists believe it is easier to achieve enlightenment once they have been reborn in the pure land.

_____

_____

_____

Activity 4.17: Achieving enlightenment in different Buddhist traditions

 pages 36–43

Six statements are given below that could be used to argue why achieving enlightenment is easier in one Buddhist tradition than another. Read these arguments and then answer the questions that follow.

1. Which branch of Buddhism does each argument apply to (Mahayana, Theravada or Pure Land)?
Write your answers underneath each argument below. One has been done for you as an example.

Argument A	Argument B	Argument C
Bodhisattvas remain in the cycle of samsara to help others achieve enlightenment.	Having faith in Amitabha is more important than a person's actions or behaviour.	Merit can be transferred to another Buddhist to help them have a favourable rebirth.
Mahayana		
Argument D	**Argument E**	**Argument F**
Everyone has the essence of a Buddha inside them (their Buddha-nature).	The Eightfold Path gives clear steps for a Buddhist to follow to achieve enlightenment.	Amitabha personally teaches Buddhists who are reborn in the pure land.

2. Which **one** of the arguments above do you think is the strongest? Explain your answer.

_____

_____

_____

_____

_____

_____

> **TIP**
>
> Which of these arguments do you think is best or worst for making the case that it is easier to achieve enlightenment in one Buddhist tradition over another?

3. Which **one** of the arguments above do you think is the weakest? Explain your answer.

_____

_____

_____

_____

_____

_____

_____

Exam practice

Use your answers to Activities 4.15–4.17 to help you write a complete answer to this exam question.

'Pure Land Buddhism is the easiest type of Buddhism in which to achieve enlightenment.' Evaluate this statement.

In your answer you should:

- refer to Buddhist teaching
- give reasoned arguments to support this statement
- give reasoned arguments to support a different point of view
- reach a justified conclusion.

> **TIP**
> The justified conclusion can agree or disagree overall with the statement, or, in some cases it can be a partial judgement. If so, make it clear why it might not be a clear-cut answer.

[12 marks]
[SPaG 3 marks]

Key Terms Glossary

As you progress through the course, you can collect the meanings of useful terms in the glossary below. You can then use the completed glossaries to revise from.

To do well in the exam you will need to understand these terms and include them in your answers. Tick the shaded circles to record how confident you feel.

Buddhahood _____

- ○ **I recognise this term**
- ◐ **I understand what this term means**
- ● **I can use this term in a sentence**

Anatta _____

The Buddha's life of luxury _____

Anicca _____

Dependent arising _____

Arhat _____

Dhamma _____

Asceticism _____

Dukkha _____

Bodhisattva _____

The Eightfold Path _____

Enlightenment

Pure Land Buddhism

The five aggregates

Sunyata

The Four Noble Truths

Theravada Buddhism

The four sights

The three marks of existence

Mahayana Buddhism

The three poisons

Nibbana

The threefold way

Chapter 5: **Buddhism: Practices**

Activity 5.1: Places of worship

pages 48–49

A Where would a Buddhist go if they wanted to carry out the following actions? Choose from the terms below, and use each term once only.

| gompa | stupa | monastery | shrine | study hall | temple |

Action	Place of worship
Attend a talk given by a Buddhist teacher	
Worship before holy relics associated with the Buddha	
Meet other Buddhists in the local community and worship together	
Meditate with other Buddhists	
Light a candle before a Buddha rupa	
Live a simple lifestyle that is dedicated to practising Buddhism full time	

B Now answer the following questions.

1. What is a Buddha rupa?

_____

_____

2. Why might a Buddhist make offerings to a Buddha rupa?

_____

_____

3. Why might a Buddhist give an offering of flowers to a Buddha rupa?

_____

Key terms

pages 50–51

Six sentences are given below about worship in Buddhism. For each sentence, replace the words in bold with the correct key term. One has been done for you as an example.

1. Buddhists carry out **acts of worship** to express gratitude and respect for the Buddha and his teachings.

Key term	*Puja*

2. Buddhists might **speak out loud scriptural passages** in order to become more receptive towards the Buddha and his teachings.

Key term	

3. Buddhists might repeat a **sequence of sacred syllables** in order to invoke the spiritual qualities of a Bodhisattva.

Key term	

4. Buddhists might use a **string of prayer beads** to help them count their recitations.

Key term	

5. Buddhists might give **things such as flowers, light or incense**. This reminds them about the Buddha's teachings.

Key term	

6. Buddhists might **sit and concentrate on one thing** in order to calm the mind and develop a greater understanding of the Buddha's teachings.

Key term	

Activity 5.2: The purpose of worship

 pages 48–51

Give **two** purposes of each of the following acts of worship. One has been done for you as an example.

Act of worship	Purpose
Making offerings at a shrine	1 _To give thanks to the Buddha for his teachings._ 2
Chanting sacred texts	1 2
Reciting a mantra	1 2

Exam practice

Now answer the following exam question.

Which one of the following is not an act of Buddhist worship?   **[1 mark]**

Put a tick (✔) in the box next to the correct answer.

A Reciting a mantra   ☐

B Meditating   ☐

C Practising asceticism   ☐

D Making an offering   ☐

Activity 5.3: Different types of meditation pages 52–59

Decide which type of meditation each of the statements below correspond to.

- If you think the statement is about samatha meditation, write 'SM' in the circle.
- If you think the statement is about vipassana meditation, write 'VM' in the circle.
- If you think the statement is about visualisation, write 'Vi' in the circle.

One has been done for you as an example.

Vi　This type of meditation requires a Buddhist to imagine an object in their mind in as much detail as possible.

This is known as calming meditation. It helps a Buddhist to calm and settle their mind.

In this type of meditation a Buddhist might switch their attention between a number of different things, including things that are more personal.

This is known as insight meditation. It helps a Buddhist to gain insight into the true nature of reality.

This type of meditation often uses a technique called mindfulness of breathing, where a Buddhist focuses all of their attention on their breathing, allowing the mind to become calm and focused.

In this type of meditation a Buddhist might use a thangka (painting) or mandala (pattern) to meditate on a Buddha, Bodhisattva or Buddhist teaching.

In this type of meditation a Buddhist might focus on a Bodhisattva in order to develop some of the characteristics associated with that Bodhisattva.

This type of meditation might be used to reflect on the three marks of existence, and to develop greater wisdom about the world.

This type of meditation might use objects (kasinas) to help focus the mind, such as water, fire or colours.

Sources of religious belief and teaching

 pages 52–59

Answer the following questions about each of the quotations.

A

> "Whenever your mind becomes scattered, use your breath as the means to take hold of your mind again."
>
> Thich Nhat Hanh, Vietnamese Buddhist Monk

1. What does this quotation suggest about the purpose of mindfulness of breathing?

_____

_____

_____

B

> "Even the gods envy those awakened and mindful ones who are intent on meditation, wise, delighting in the peace of the absence of desire."
>
> The Buddha in the *Dhammapada*, verse 181

1. Give **three** benefits of meditation suggested by this quotation.

1 _____

_____

2 _____

_____

3 _____

_____

C

> "Think of morality, concentrated meditation, and wisdom as a blueprint for enlightenment, reminding us of the highest aim of practice – a transformation of attitude toward peacefulness, compassion, calm focus, and wisdom."
>
> Tenzin Gyatso, 14th Dalai Lama

1. Briefly explain how the following three types of meditation each contribute to the 'transformation of attitude' that the Dalai Lama outlines above.

Samatha meditation: _____

_____

Vipassana meditation: _____

_____

Visualisation: _____

_____

Exam practice

Use your answers to the previous two activities to write an answer to this exam question.

Explain **two** reasons why meditation is important for Buddhists.

Refer to sacred writings or another source of Buddhist belief and teaching in your answer.

[5 marks]

_____

_____

_____

_____

_____

_____

_____

_____

_____

_____

_____

_____

_____

Activity 5.4: Ceremonies and rituals associated with death and mourning

 pages 60–61

Six practices associated with death and mourning in Buddhism are given below. Which of the following Buddhist traditions is each practice associated with?

- Theravada Buddhism
- Tibetan Buddhism
- Japanese Buddhism

One has been done for you as an example.

The deceased is placed in a coffin with their head pointing west, towards Sukhavati.	_Japanese_
A traditional practice is 'sky burial', where the body is left in a high place in the mountains as a gift to the vultures.	
Revered teachers are cremated and their remains are placed inside stupas. These often become pilgrimage sites for Buddhists today.	
Family and friends perform actions that transfer merit to the deceased, such as donating to a charity.	
After the cremation it is common for relatives to pick out the bones from the ashes using chopsticks.	
Monks often attend the funeral of a lay person to give a sermon and perform Buddhist rites.	

Activity 5.5: How Buddhist teachings link to death and mourning pages 60–61

Answer the following questions about death and mourning.

1. Buddhist tradition teaches that when a Buddhist dies, their kammic energy leaves their body and is reborn in a new one. How favourable this rebirth is depends on the actions the person took during their lifetime.

   How is this teaching reflected in Theravada funerals?

   _____

   _____

   _____

   _____

   _____

2. How might the teaching of anicca help a Buddhist to overcome their grief when a loved one dies?

   _____

   _____

   _____

   _____

   _____

   _____

   _____

3. In Pure Land Buddhism, the coffin is placed so it points towards the west, and the mourners chant Amitabha's name as they process around it. What do you think is the purpose or meaning of these two practices?

   _____

   _____

   _____

   _____

   _____

   _____

   _____

Activity 5.6: The importance of ceremonies and rituals associated with death and mourning

pages 60–61

Add to the spider diagram below to give at least **five** different reasons why ceremonies and rituals associated with death and mourning are important to Buddhists. An example has been given for you.

TIP
Think of both the deceased and the living.

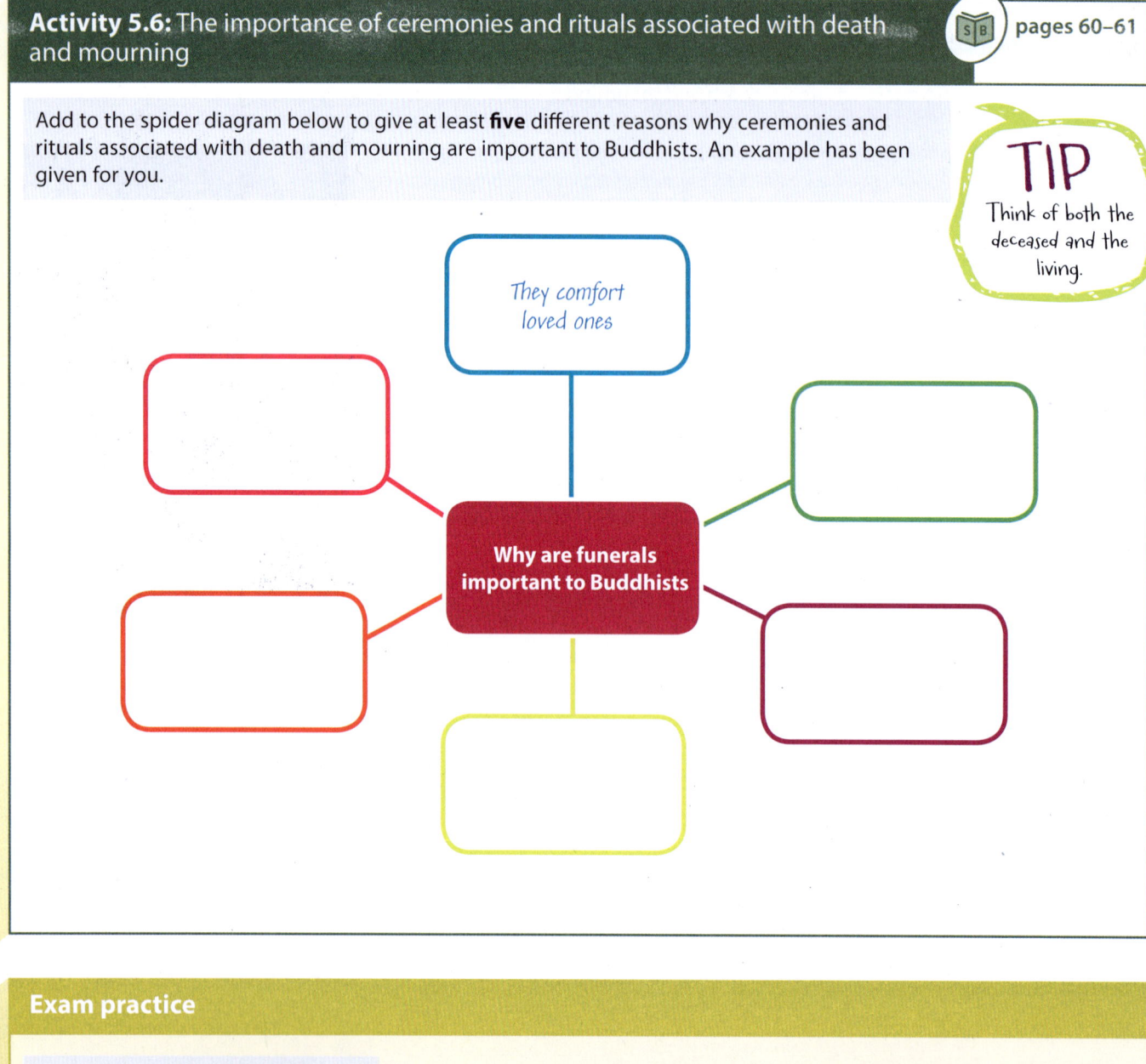

They comfort loved ones

Why are funerals important to Buddhists

Exam practice

Now answer this exam question.

Explain **two** contrasting Buddhist funeral practices. **[4 marks]**

_____

_____

_____

_____

_____

_____

_____

_____

_____

TIP
Remember that 'contrasting' simply means 'different'.

Activity 5.7: Worship in the home or in the temple?

 pages 48–61

A Here are three arguments for and three arguments against the statement, 'Temples are vital in Buddhism'. In the table below, identify and number the arguments that support the statement. Then identify and number the arguments that directly oppose each point of view.

Argument 1

The temple may house specific and unique aids to worship that a Buddhist can use during their devotional practice, such as thangkas and mandalas.

Argument 2

The temple allows access to Buddhist monks and nuns – they can teach and explain the Dhamma to the lay congregation.

Argument 3

Actions outside the temple can also produce positive kammic merit. For example, maintaining a shrine at home is an action which allows for the accumulation of positive kamma.

Argument 4

There are many websites that help to explain the Buddha's teachings. In addition, the development of technology means that Buddhists can watch and listen to monks from their own home.

Argument 5

Temples allow Buddhists to perform actions which produce positive kammic merit, such as offering food to the monastic community.

Argument 6

There are no prescribed procedures or aids to worship needed in Buddhism. Buddhists aim to live their lives as Buddha lived his and to embrace of all of his practices. These practices did not happen in a Temple.

One argument that supports the statement is:	
An argument that disagrees with this point of view is:	
A second argument that supports the statement is:	
An argument that disagrees with this point of view is:	
A third argument that supports the statement is:	
An argument that disagrees with this point of view is:	

B The statement above is similar to a statement for a 12-mark question. Consider the arguments above to decide whether you agree or disagree with the statement, 'Temples are vital in Buddhism'. Explain your reasoning below to help you reach a justified conclusion.

I agree/disagree with the statement because:

_____

_____

_____

_____

_____

I am not persuaded by the alternative argument because:

_____

_____

_____

_____

Activity 5.8: The importance of festivals and retreats   pages 62–63

Complete the boxes below to give **three** more reasons why festivals and retreats are important to Buddhists. Support each reason with an example from a specific festival or retreat. One has been done for you.

Reason:	Example:
Festivals help Buddhists to reflect on the Buddha's teachings.	*Parinirvana Day encourages Buddhists to focus on the teaching of impermanence.*

Activity 5.9: Wesak and Parinirvana Day

 pages 62–63

Fill in the middle column of this table.

- For the first section you should explain what the **difference** is between the two terms on either side.

- For the last section you should explain what the **link** is between the two terms or phrases on either side.

	Explain the difference between the two terms	
Festival		Retreat
Wesak		Parinirvana Day

	Explain the link between the two terms or phrases	
Wesak		Light
Parinirvana Day		Pilgrimage
Releasing birds from cages in Singapore to symbolise liberation		Lighting giant paper lanterns in Indonesia to symbolise overcoming ignorance
Reading and studying the *Mahaparinirvana Sutra*		Reflecting on the impermanent nature of reality

Activity 5.10: Festivals in Buddhism pages 62–63

Answer the following questions about festivals.

1. In the boxes below give **one** argument for and **one** argument against the idea that festivals are the best way to remember the life and teachings of the Buddha.

For:	Against:

2. According to the 2011 census, only 0.4% of England's population identified as Buddhist. Therefore, Buddhism can be considered a minority religion in England. Given the status of Buddhism, what issues do you think Buddhists might face when celebrating their festivals in England today?

_____

_____

_____

_____

_____

_____

3. How does the following source of religious belief and teaching link to the celebration of Wesak and Parinirvana Day?

> ❝All conditioned phenomena are impermanent.❞
> The Buddha in the *Dhammapada,* verse 277

_____

_____

_____

_____

_____

_____

Activity 5.11: Buddhist teachings about kamma

 pages 64–65

A Fill in the gaps in the sentences below.

The Buddhist principle that explains how a person's decisions and actions lead to happiness or suffering is

called k_____ .

For Buddhists, there are two types of action. S_____ actions lead to happiness and

are rooted in generosity, compassion and understanding. In contrast, u_____ actions

are rooted in c_____ , hatred and ignorance, and these lead to s_____ .

The principle of kamma teaches that Buddhists can change their own f_____ through

their own actions. It encourages Buddhists to act in an e_____ way, as this will increase

their own and others' happiness.

B Use your answers to the first half of this activity to help explain the following quotation.
What does the Buddha mean? How does this quotation relate to the principle of kamma?

> **❝**what we are today comes from our thoughts of yesterday, and our present thoughts build our life of tomorrow **❞**
>
> The Buddha in the *Dhammapada*, verse 1

TIP
Remember that 'thoughts' are important to the idea of kamma because they lead directly to actions.

_____

_____

_____

_____

_____

_____

_____

_____

_____

_____

_____

_____

_____

Activity 5.12: Kamma and rebirth

 pages 64–65

In the book *The Questions of King Milinda*, the teacher Nagasena uses the following analogy to explain the concept of rebirth. He compares rebirth to the act of lighting a wick on one candle with the flame of another. Although not the same flame, it has originated because of the first.

Answer the following questions about kamma and rebirth.

1. How do you think this analogy links to the concept of rebirth in Buddhism?

_____

_____

_____

_____

_____

2. Give **one** strength of this analogy as a way of helping to explain the concept of rebirth.

_____

_____

_____

_____

3. Give **one** weakness of this analogy as a way of helping to explain the concept of rebirth.

_____

_____

_____

_____

4. How do you think the concepts of kamma and rebirth might affect a Buddhist's ethical conduct? Explain your answer.

_____

_____

_____

_____

_____

_____

Exam practice

Now answer this exam question.

Give **two** Buddhist teachings about kamma.   **[2 marks]**

1 _____

_____

2 _____

_____

Activity 5.13: Compassion and loving-kindness   pages 66–69

A Tick the correct boxes to show whether the following statements are true or false.

	True	False
The feeling of compassion encourages Buddhists to take practical steps to help relieve the suffering of others.	☐	☐
Loving-kindness means showing an attitude of warmth and kindness towards others.	☐	☐
Buddhists should show compassion to themselves as well as others.	☐	☐
Buddhists should only show others loving-kindness if they receive it themselves.	☐	☐
The Bodhisattva Avalokitesvara represents compassion.	☐	☐
Samatha meditation specifically aims to help Buddhists develop an attitude of loving-kindness.	☐	☐
Cultivating compassion is essential for becoming a Bodhisattva.	☐	☐

B For the statements you have marked as 'false', write one or two sentences with the correct information.

_____

_____

_____

_____

_____

_____

Activity 5.14: Compassion and loving-kindness in practice   pages 66–69

Answer the following questions about compassion and loving-kindness.

1. Why might some people argue that it is not possible to show compassion and loving-kindness at all times to all people?

    _____

    _____

    _____

2. How do you think a Buddhist might respond to this argument?

    _____

    _____

    _____

3. Given your understanding of compassion and loving-kindness, what do you think a Buddhist might feel about the three situations described below? Would they approve or disapprove of each one? Why?

Situation	Would a Buddhist approve/disapprove? Why?
Volunteering at a local food bank	
Feeling angry towards a friend you recently had an argument with	
Feeling sad that a cyclone has devastated many homes in another country	

4. The Buddha and Dalai Lama have said the following about compassion and loving-kindness:

    > ❝ [He] who wishes to attain that state of calm (nibbana)… let him radiate boundless love towards the entire world. ❞
    >
    > The Buddha in the *Karaniya Metta Sutta*, verse 150

    > ❝ The key to a happier and more successful world is the growth of compassion. ❞
    >
    > Tenzin Gyatso, 14th Dalai Lama

    What do these two quotations teach about why it is important to develop the attitudes of loving-kindness and compassion?

    _____

    _____

    _____

    _____

Activity 5.15: The five moral precepts

  pages 70–71

Answer the following questions about the five moral precepts.

1. Which of the five moral precepts is each of the following actions breaking?

Action	Precept
Exploiting workers who are desperate for jobs by paying them very little	
Eating meat	
Drinking wine	
Committing adultery	
Gossiping about the bad choices that a friend has made	

2. Which **one** of the five moral precepts do you think a Buddhist would find easiest to follow? Give a reason for your answer.

_____

_____

_____

_____

3. Which **one** of the five moral precepts do you think a Buddhist would find hardest to follow? Give a reason for your answer.

_____

_____

_____

_____

4. Buddhists do not believe they will be 'punished' by a god if they do not follow the five moral precepts. Why then is it important for Buddhists to follow the five moral precepts?

_____

_____

_____

5. Buddhism teaches that the precepts need to be applied sensitively. Give **two** situations where a Buddhist might consider it best to break one of the precepts.

1 _____

_____

_____

2 _____

_____

_____

TIP

Abortion and speaking truthfully are two areas where Buddhists might want to break one of the precepts.

Activity 5.16: The six perfections

SB   pages 72–73

Each of the actions below describes one of the six perfections. Label each action with the correct perfection.

generosity or giving   morality   patience   energy   meditation   wisdom

Action	Perfection
Meditating regularly to develop concentration and awareness	
Studying the Buddha's teachings to gain insight into the nature of reality	
Following the five moral precepts	
Donating clothes to those in need	
Enduring and accepting suffering as an inevitable part of life	
Speaking kindly about others rather than talking about their faults	
Putting effort and enthusiasm into practising the Buddha's teachings	
Teaching the Dhamma to the younger generation	

Activity 5.17: Living ethically in Buddhism

pages 64–73

Answer the following questions on living ethically in Buddhism.

1. What do you think it means to live 'ethically'?

_____

_____

_____

_____

2. Explain how an understanding of the following can help a Buddhist to live an ethical life.

Buddhist teaching	How does this help Buddhists to live ethically?
Kamma	
Compassion and loving-kindness	
The five moral precepts	
The six perfections	

Exam practice

Use your answers to Activities 5.15-5.17 to help you answer this exam question.

'The five moral precepts are all Buddhists need to live an ethical life.'

Evaluate this statement.

In your answer you should:

- refer to Buddhist teaching
- give reasoned arguments to support this statement
- give reasoned arguments to support a different point of view
- reach a justified conclusion.

[12 marks]

TIP

Your answer should have logical chains of reasoning. One way to achieve this is to think of it like a debate where different views are presented and evaluated, by taking turns in an organised way.

Key Terms Glossary

As you progress through the course, you can collect the meanings of useful terms in the glossary below. You can then use the completed glossaries to revise from.

To do well in the exam you will need to understand these terms and include them in your answers. Tick the shaded circles to record how confident you feel. Use the extra boxes at the end to record any other terms that you have found difficult, along with their definitions.

○ **I recognise this term**

◐ **I understand what this term means**

● **I can use this term in a sentence**

Buddha rupa

Chanting

Compassion

Festival

The five moral precepts

Gompa

Kamma

Loving-kindness

Mala

Mantra

Meditation

Mindfulness of breathing

Retreat

Monastery

Samatha meditation

Offerings

Shrine

Parinirvana Day

The six perfections

Puja

Stupa

Rebirth

Temple

Vipassana meditation

Visualisation

Wesak

Worship

Test the 1-mark question

Example

1 Which **one** of the following best describes someone who has attained enlightenment? **[1 mark]**

Put a tick (✔) in the box next to the correct answer.

A Bodhisattva ✔

B Buddhist

C Ascetic

D Monk ✔ **(1)**

WHAT WILL THE QUESTION LOOK LIKE?

The 1-mark question will always be a **multiple-choice question** with four answers to choose from. Only one answer is correct. The question will usually start with the words **'Which one of the following…'**.

HOW IS IT MARKED?

You will receive 1 mark for choosing the correct answer by putting a tick in the box next to this answer. You do not need to explain your choice and you must not select more than one answer.

(!) REMEMBER…

Read the question and all of the options **carefully** before selecting your answer. The main reason why marks are lost for this question is because this has not been done.

Many of the 1-mark questions will test you on the **meaning of religious terms** from the specification, so try to learn all of these words.

Activity

2 Which **one** of the following is **not** one of the six perfections? **[1 mark]**

Put a tick (✔) in the box next to the correct answer.

A Patience

B Morality

C Meditation

D Love

3 Which **one** of the following is one of the threefold ways? **[1 mark]**

Put a tick (✔) in the box next to the correct answer.

A Ahimsa

B Metta

C Wisdom

D Puja

TIP

Try to ensure that you know the meaning of all the terms listed on the specification. You could be asked questions on any of these terms in the exam.

Test the 2-mark question

Example

1 | Give **two** different types of Buddhist meditation. **[2 marks]**

Samatha ✔ *(1)*

Vipassana ✔ *(1)*

REMEMBER…

Write your answer on **two separate lines**. This will help you to remember that you need to give **two pieces of information**, each of which should be different.

Keep your answers short. You only need to provide two facts or short ideas; **you don't need to explain them or express any opinions**.

Activity

2 | Give **two** Buddhist teachings about the concept of dependent arising. **[2 marks]**

The sample answer below would get 1 mark because only one answer is correct. Put a line through the sentence that would not get any marks and then add a new point for a second mark.

Everything is constantly changing.

Suffering is a part of life.

_____

_____

3 | Give **two** of the four sights. **[2 marks]**

1 _____

_____

2 _____

_____

4 | Name **two** festivals celebrated by Buddhists. **[2 marks]**

1 _____

_____

2 _____

_____

TIP
Try not to spend too much time on these questions. Ideally you should spend a maximum of 2 minutes on a 2-mark question.

Test the 4-mark question

Example

1 Explain **two** contrasting ways a Buddhist might remember the life of the Buddha. **[4 marks]**

One way is by performing pilgrimage. ✓ **(1)** *For example they may visit Bodh Gaya where the Buddha became enlightened by meditating under the Bodhi tree.* ✓ **(1)**

Another way is by celebrating Wesak. ✓ **(1)** *This festival remembers three major events in the Buddha's life.* ✓ **(1)**

! REMEMBER...

Make **two different points**. Try to show the examiner where each point begins. For example, start your answer with 'One way is…' and then move on to your second point by saying 'Another way is…'.

Try to **develop** each point with an example or more explanation. Developing your points will earn you more marks.

WHAT WILL THE QUESTION LOOK LIKE?

The 4-mark question will always start with the words **'Explain two…'**, and a maximum of **4 marks** will be awarded. You are asked to 'Explain', which means you will need to show **development** of ideas.

HOW IS IT MARKED?

You will be awarded 1 mark for each point and 1 mark for the development of each point. This answer would gain 4 marks because it makes two different points, and both points are clearly developed.

Activity

2 Explain **two** ways the Eightfold Path may influence a Buddhist today. **[4 marks]**

The sample answer below would get 4 marks because there are two carefully developed points. Add a tick next to each point. Then underline where each point has been developed.

One way is that it may encourage them to perform 'right actions'. This means a Buddhist will perform actions that cause no harm to others, including humans and animals.

Another way is that it may influence them to perform 'right speech'. This means a Buddhist will avoid lying, gossiping or saying hurtful things about others.

TIP

The 4-mark question in the 'Beliefs' section of your exam paper will ask you about how an event or teaching in Buddhism has influenced something else.

3 Explain **two** ways in which the Buddha's life of luxury influenced his teachings. **[4 marks]**

The following sample answer would get 2 marks giving two different ways. Develop each point to gain 2 more marks.

One way is that it helped to develop his teaching of 'the middle way.' ✓ **(1)**

_____

_____

_____

Another way is that it influenced his teaching that Buddhists should not become attached to material pleasures. ✔ *(1)*

_____

_____

_____

4 | Explain **two** contrasting ways that Buddhists can practise the five moral precepts.   **[4 marks]**

_____

_____

_____

_____

_____

_____

_____

_____

_____

TIP

In the 'Practices' section of the exam paper, the 4-mark question will ask you to explain **two contrasting ways** in which a practice is carried out. Remember that 'contrasting' simply means 'different'.

5 | Explain **two** ways that Pure Land Buddhism may influence Buddhists today.   **[4 marks]**

_____

_____

_____

_____

_____

_____

_____

_____

_____

_____

_____

Test the 5-mark question

Example

1 Explain **two** teachings about the Buddha's early life.

Refer to sacred writings or another source of Buddhist belief and teaching in your answer. **[5 marks]**

One teaching is that the Buddha had a miraculous birth. ✓ **(1)**
For example it is said that he could walk and talk as soon as he was born. ✓ **(1)**

Another teaching is that the Buddha was sheltered from everything that caused suffering. ✓ **(1)** *This is because the Buddha's father wanted the Buddha to become a king, not a holy man.* ✓ **(1)**
For example, the Jataka tales teach that it was not until the Buddha was a young man that he first saw the sights of illness, old age and death. ✓ **(1)**

WHAT WILL THE QUESTION LOOK LIKE?

The 5-mark question will always start with the words **'Explain two…'** and end with the words **'Refer to sacred writings or another source of Buddhist belief and teaching in your answer'**. A maximum of **5 marks** will be awarded.

HOW IS IT MARKED?

This answer would gain 5 marks because it makes two different points, and both points are clearly developed. It also refers to a relevant source of Buddhist belief and teaching, which gains 1 more mark.

! REMEMBER…

The 5-mark question is similar to the 4-mark question, so try to make **two different points** and **develop** each of them.

The additional instruction in the question asks you to **'refer to sacred writings or another source of Buddhist belief and teaching in your answer'**. Try to think of a reference to a religious text (such as the Dhammapada) or a Buddhist teacher (such as the Dalai Lama). You only need one reference.

Activity

2 Explain **two** reasons why meditation is important for Buddhists.

Refer to sacred writings or another source of Buddhist belief and teaching in your answer. **[5 marks]**

The sample answer below would get 5 marks because there are two developed points and a reference to a source of Buddhist belief and teaching. Add a tick next to each point. Then underline where each point has been developed. Finally, draw a circle around the reference to Buddhist belief and teaching.

One reason is because by meditating Buddhists are following the Buddha's teaching. In the Dhammapada it says the Buddha taught his followers to use meditation to overcome Mara's fetter. This means that to overcome craving and free themselves from the cycle of samsara Buddhists should engage in meditation.

Another reason is because it allows Buddhists to cultivate positive attitudes. For example, during metta meditation, Buddhists try to cultivate the attitude of loving-kindness.

TIP

For the 5-mark question you do not need to learn and give word-for-word quotations from sacred writings or religious teachers. For example, here the student has simply referred to a detail in the Dhammapada; this is enough to gain a mark.

3 Explain **two** of the six perfections.

Refer to sacred writings or another source of Buddhist belief and teaching in your answer. **[5 marks]**

> **"** Give, even if you only have a little. **"**
>
> The Buddha in the *Dhammapada*, verse 224

> **"** It is possible to abandon what is unskilful. **"**
>
> The Buddha in the *Kusala Sutta*, verse 19

> **"** Whenever your mind becomes scattered, use your breath as the means to take hold of your mind again. **"**
>
> Thich Nhat Hanh, Vietnamese Buddhist monk

> **"** Even the gods envy those awakened and mindful ones who are intent on meditation. **"**
>
> The Buddha in the *Dhammapada*, verse 181

Four quotations are given above. Use **one** of these quotations to complete the answer that follows, which needs a reference to sacred writings or another source of Buddhist belief and teaching. You can add this reference to either the first point or the second point.

The perfection of generosity means a Buddhist will give whatever they can to help others overcome suffering. This might include material goods, protection from fear, or the Buddha's teachings.

_____

_____

_____

_____

The perfection of meditation means a Buddhist will engage in samatha meditation. They might do this by using mindfulness of breathing to calm the mind.

_____

_____

_____

_____

TIP

Make sure that any source of Buddhist belief and teaching you use is relevant to the point you are making. This means it should support or back-up the point or argument you are trying to make.

4 Explain **two** Buddhist teachings about the human personality.

Refer to sacred writings or another source of Buddhist belief and teaching in your answer. **[5 marks]**

Four sentence starters are given below. Use **two** of these to write a complete answer to this question. You will need to develop both of these points and also refer to sacred writings or another source of Buddhist belief and teaching to gain full marks.

Theravada Buddhism teaches that people are made of five aggregates...

One Buddhist teaching is that people do not have a 'soul' or 'self'...

An important teaching in Mahayana Buddhism about the human personality is the teaching of sunyata...

One Buddhist teaching is that everyone has a Buddha-nature...

_____

_____

_____

_____

_____

_____

_____

_____

_____

_____

_____

TIP

Words or phrases that you could use to develop your answers include 'this means that', 'for example', 'because' or 'as a result'.

5 Explain **two** reasons why Parinirvana Day is important to Buddhists.

Refer to sacred writings or another source of Buddhist belief and teaching in your answer.   **[5 marks]**

_____

_____

_____

_____

_____

_____

_____

_____

_____

_____

_____

6 Explain **two** Buddhist teachings about the concept of dependent arising.

Refer to sacred writings or another source of Buddhist belief and teaching in your answer.   **[5 marks]**

_____

_____

_____

_____

_____

_____

_____

_____

_____

_____

_____

_____

7 Explain **two** reasons why the Four Noble Truths are important for Buddhists today.

Refer to sacred writings or another source of Buddhist belief and teaching in your answer. **[5 marks]**

Test the 12-mark question

Example

1 'The first noble truth is the most important.'

Evaluate this statement.

In your answer you should:

- refer to Buddhist teaching
- give reasoned arguments to support this statement
- give reasoned arguments to support a different point of view
- reach a justified conclusion.

[12 marks]
[SPaG 3 marks]

WHAT WILL THE QUESTION LOOK LIKE?

The 12-mark question will always ask you to **evaluate** a statement. The bullet points underneath the statement will tell you the things the examiner expects to see in your answer. Here, it says you need to 'refer to Buddhist teaching', so make sure you write about core Buddhist beliefs and include important sources of religious belief and teaching. You also need to give reasoned arguments to support two different points of view. The final bullet point will always ask you to 'reach a justified conclusion'.

HOW IS IT MARKED?

The examiner will mark your answer using a mark scheme based on level descriptors, similar to the one opposite.

In the 'Beliefs' section of the exam paper, you will also be assessed on the quality of your written communication in the 12-mark question. A maximum of 3 marks will be awarded for accurate **spelling, punctuation and grammar** as well as the use of a range of **specialist terms**. Allow yourself time in the exam to check that you have done this in your answer.

! REMEMBER...

To evaluate the statement, you need to have:

- A paragraph or paragraphs in support of the statement which explain why some people might agree with the statement, and give reasons (including Buddhist views) to support this.
- A paragraph or paragraphs opposing the statement which explain, why other people might disagree with the statement and give reasons (including Buddhist views) to support this view.
- A justified conclusion which explains which side of the argument you think has the strongest evidence, briefly referring to the evidence as you write. You should explain why you think this is the strongest evidence/argument in support or in opposition of the statement.

What might make a strong argument?

- Based on a religious teaching/source of authority
- Based on scientific evidence
- The majority of Buddhists accept it

What might make a weak argument?

- Based on personal opinion rather than religious teaching
- A popular idea that has no scientific basis
- Very few Buddhists would agree with it

Level descriptors

Level 4 (10–12 marks)	• A well-argued response, reasoned consideration of different points of view. • Logical chains of reasoning leading to judgement(s) supported by knowledge and understanding of relevant evidence and information. • **Reference to religion applied to the issue.**
Level 3 (7–9 marks)	• Reasoned consideration of different points of view. • Logical chains of reasoning that draw on knowledge and understanding of relevant evidence and information. • **Clear reference to religion.**
Level 2 (4–6 marks)	• Reasoned consideration of a point of view. • A logical chain of reasoning drawing on knowledge and understanding of relevant evidence and information. OR • Recognition of different points of view, each supported by relevant reasons / evidence. • **Maximum of Level 2 if there is no reference to religion.**
Level 1 (1–3 marks)	• Point of view with reason(s) stated in support.

Here are four sample answers to the example question opposite. Each answer would be awarded a different Level. Read through the answers to get an idea of what a Level 1, 2, 3 or 4 answer looks like.

Level 1 sample answer

This is a Level 1 answer because:

- it only gives a point of view for one side of the argument
- it only gives a basic reason for this point of view which is not developed
- it shows a very limited understanding of Buddhism
- there is no conclusion.

To improve this answer the student could:

- develop the point of view they have stated
- include more teachings from Buddhism
- include a developed point of view for the other side of the argument
- reach a justified conclusion explaining whether the argument is strong or weak.

It is the most important because it is the first one. It is the reason all the others exist, they follow on from this one. Without the Buddha teaching the first one, what would be the point of the other three?

TIP

'It is the reason all the others exist' is a good point but it is not developed. To develop the idea the student could explain *why* the first truth is the reason the other truths exist. How does the first truth influence the other three?

Level 2 sample answer

This is a Level 2 answer because:

- it refers to different arguments for and against the statement, which have some development
- it refers to some teachings in Buddhism
- it comes to a conclusion about which side is correct.

To improve this answer the student could:

- develop the different arguments linked to the statement with relevant evidence
- include more reference to relevant teachings within Buddhism
- develop the conclusion to explain why one argument is stronger than the other.

The first noble truth is the most important because it highlights the idea of suffering. If this truth is accepted by Buddhists, they will be able to understand the world around them a bit better and get more out of the other three truths. But it is also not true that it is the most important because it is not really saying anything new. Even without the teaching of the Buddha, people can see suffering and unhappiness around them. In conclusion, I disagree with the statement because the other truths help a Buddhist more.

TIP
This student has begun to explain the reasons for their view. This is an essential part of a 12-mark answer.

Level 3 sample answer

This is a Level 3 answer because:

- it has developed relevant arguments for and against the statement
- it refers to relevant Buddhist teachings
- it comes to a brief, reasoned consideration of the points of view in the conclusion.

To improve this answer the student could:

- provide more relevant development or detail in their arguments for and against the statement
- include more detailed reference to relevant teachings within Buddhism
- give a more justified conclusion where all of the elements presented in the answer are judged.

In this essay I am going to discuss why some people agree that the first noble truth is the most important and why other people disagree that the first noble truth is the most important.

Many Buddhists will agree that the first noble truth is the most important. This is because the first noble truth teaches that dukkha (suffering) exists and is a part of life that can't be avoided. When Buddhists realise suffering exists they can work on overcoming it which is the point of the other three noble truths. This means that Buddhists have to accept the first noble truth before they can move on to the other three, so it is the most important.

However, some Buddhists may disagree and say that the first truth isn't the most important, actually the fourth truth is the most important. This is because the first truth is very obvious – if you look around the world it is clear to see suffering. But the fourth truth is more practical because it teaches Buddhists how to overcome suffering with eight steps on the Eightfold Path. The Buddha teaches it is like a 'cure' for suffering.

In conclusion, I disagree with the statement because the first noble truth doesn't really help Buddhists in any way but the fourth noble truth does.

TIP
You don't need to include an introduction in your answer – just go straight into the arguments for or against the statement.

TIP
It is a good idea to start a new paragraph when you give a different point of view.

TIP
Using phrases such as 'however', 'in contrast' or 'others disagree because' will help to show the examiner you are offering a contrasting opinion.

TIP
The student has mentioned relevant teachings from the Buddha, who is a source of authority for all Buddhists. This shows a 'clear reference to religion'.

Level 4 sample answer

This is a Level 4 answer because:

- there are developed reasons for and against the statement which are fully relevant
- there is accurate and detailed reference to relevant teachings within Buddhism
- it is clear the student knows a lot about the topic, and the whole answer is clearly linked to the statement
- there is a justified conclusion which makes a judgement about which side is stronger based on relevant evidence and information.

Many Buddhists may agree that the first noble truth is the most important because without understanding that dukkha exists, they will not understand the purpose of the Buddha's teachings. Many Buddhists compare the Buddha to a physician and the Four Noble Truths to medicine. It therefore makes sense for Buddhists to accept the first noble truth as the most important because if the Buddha is to 'cure' the world, Buddhists must first diagnose the illness. This is the purpose of the first noble truth, which teaches that the 'illness' is the presence and existence of suffering. In the Dhammapada the Buddha teaches that "all conditioned phenomena are dukkha", which basically means that everything can cause suffering. The Buddha developed these ideas further by suggesting that suffering is caused by pain, change and attachment. Once the first noble truth is accepted, Buddhists can use the other truths to overcome suffering. Therefore, for many Buddhists the first noble truth is the most important.

Yet other Buddhists may disagree. They may suggest that it is obvious to see that the world is full of suffering therefore making the first noble truth just a common-sense statement, the important and meaningful dhamma is found in the three other truths, these are what really help Buddhists overcome dukkha. Some Buddhists may argue that the fourth noble truth is the most important because it gives eight practical and accessible ways for a Buddhist to overcome dukkha and achieve nibbana. The Buddha teaches the Eightfold Path, taught within the fourth noble truth allows for the "abandoning of the unwholesome". Therefore, due to its practicality and applicability some Buddhists argue the fourth, not the first noble truth, is the most important.

In conclusion, I do not agree with the statement. Rather, I find the arguments which suggest the fourth noble truth is more important than the first, more convincing. This is because contained within the fourth noble truth is the Buddha's 'middle way' achieved by following the Eightfold Path. Specific actions are prescribed to Buddhists, e.g. right meditation, right action, right speech and right livelihood; all together this provides Buddhists with a structure, purpose and means to live their life by; this is far more useful and insightful than a simple examination of the world offered by the first noble truth.

TIP

This is a very well-structured response with a clear line of reasoning that leads to a justified conclusion. It is worthwhile spending a bit of time planning your own response. Start by thinking of arguments for and against the statement. Think of evidence you could use to support this. Remember to end with a justified conclusion, stating which side you find more convincing and explain why you think this.

TIP

This student would gain all 3 SPaG marks as their spelling, punctuation and grammar are accurate and they have used specialist terms like 'dukkha', 'Dhammapada' and 'enlightenment'.

TIP

Try to use accurate and relevant sources of religious belief and teaching to support the points you are making.

Activity

2 'Celebrating Parinirvana Day is the best way for Buddhists to remember the Buddha's teaching.'

Evaluate this statement.

In your answer you should:

- refer to Buddhist teaching
- give reasoned arguments to support this statement
- give reasoned arguments to support a different point of view
- reach a justified conclusion. **[12 marks]**

A Read the sample answer below.

Some Buddhists will agree with the statement as Parinirvana Day helps them to focus on a central teaching of the Buddha, which is anicca. This teaching encapsulates the Buddha's understanding of the nature of reality, it is one of the three marks of existence, the Buddha suggested "All conditioned phenomena are impermanent", this means that everything (including people, objects and emotions) is always changing, and nothing remains the same. This is an important teaching for many Buddhists as it helps them overcome and accept the dukkha associated with death. This is particularly relevant for Buddhists on Parinirvana Day, as a focus of the festival is giving Buddhists the opportunity to reflect upon death, both the death of their loved ones and their own mortality. They may do this through meditation, puja and/or by reading the Mahaparinirvana Sutra to learn more about the Buddha's death.

However, other Buddhists will disagree because Parinirvana Day is not celebrated by all Buddhists, it is a festival mainly celebrated by Mahayana Buddhism, some may therefore claim it excludes other Buddhists e.g. Theravada Buddhists. They may argue, how can a festival which excludes most of the Buddhist community be the best way for Buddhists to remember the Buddha's teaching? Moreover, the festival has a very narrow focus, it therefore doesn't allow Buddhists to remember the Buddha's Dhamma in its entirety, he taught much more than anicca! In contrast the Pali Canon is an important source of authority for nearly all Buddhists and it discusses lots of different aspects of the Buddha's teaching, like the four noble truths and how to reach enlightenment, so some Buddhists may claim that reading this is a better way to remember the Buddha's teaching.

Overall, I disagree with the statement. I think the best way to remember the Buddha's teaching is by reading scripture. I think scripture is a much better way because of the depth of their teaching e.g. the Pali Canon teaches topics such as the Buddha's life, monastic rules and philosophical insight. Additionally, scripture is always available to Buddhists, e.g. at the temple, via the Internet etc., rather than waiting for the yearly occurrence of a festival.

B Now answer the following questions about the sample answer above.

1. The student makes one main argument to support the statement. What is it?

_____

_____

_____

_____

2. How do they develop this point?

_____

_____

_____

_____

_____

3. The student makes one main argument against the statement. What is it?

_____

_____

_____

_____

4. How do they develop this point?

_____

_____

_____

_____

_____

5. The question says you should 'refer to Buddhist teaching'. Using a coloured pen, highlight any references to Buddhist teaching that you can find.

6. The student uses a range of specialist terms. Write examples of these terms below.

_____

_____

_____

7. The question asks you to 'reach a justified conclusion'. Circle the sentence where the student gives their judgement. Then underline the sentence where they summarise their evidence.

8. Can you find and highlight in a different coloured pen any phrases which show the student is evaluating their arguments?

3 'Visualisation is the most important type of meditation.'

Evaluate this statement.

In your answer you should:

- refer to Buddhist teaching
- give reasoned arguments to support this statement
- give reasoned arguments to support a different point of view
- reach a justified conclusion. **[12 marks]**

Read the sample answer below.

This is a Level 2 answer. **Rewrite it so it gains a Level 3 or, if possible, a Level 4.**
To make it a Level 3 answer you need to:

- ensure you have different points of view which are developed and supported by relevant knowledge
- refer to relevant Buddhist teachings
- show a brief, reasoned consideration of the points of view in the conclusion.

To make it a Level 4 answer you also need to:

- include developed reasons for and against the statement which are fully relevant
- make accurate and detailed references to teachings within Buddhism
- justify the conclusion by making a judgement about which side is stronger based on relevant evidence and information.

In this essay I am going to argue that visualisation is the most important type of meditation. Some Buddhists may agree with this statement because they use meditation to help them become a Bodhisattva. So by imaging a picture of a Bodhisattva they will become more like the Bodhisattva themselves. They might focus on somebody who is compassionate so they can become more compassionate. If they want to become a Bodhisattva this is the best type of meditation to use.

4 'Everyone can become enlightened.'

Evaluate this statement.

In your answer you should:

- refer to Buddhist teaching
- give reasoned arguments to support this statement
- give reasoned arguments to support a different point of view
- reach a justified conclusion.

[12 marks]
[SPaG 3 marks]

Here is the beginning of a response to the question above, which gives some arguments in support of the statement. To complete the answer you need to give developed arguments against the statement and reach a justified conclusion.

Complete the answer below.

- Begin your first paragraph with the sentence, 'However, some Buddhists would disagree with the statement because…'.
- Include reference to Buddhist teachings.
- Finally, add a justified conclusion. This could begin, 'After considering both sides of the argument, the most convincing position is…'.

Some Mahayana Buddhists will agree with this statement as they believe that everyone has a Buddha-nature inside them. This means that anyone can realise the Buddha within them and become enlightened if they practise the six perfections. The Chinese Buddhist teacher Huineng compared the realisation process to a moon being obscured by clouds, and once the clouds have dropped away the moon is revealed. So by following the Buddha's teachings, such as by practising meditation and the five moral precepts, anyone has the ability to get rid of the 'clouds' (their desires, attachments and ignorance) and reveal the 'moon' (become enlightened). As these practices are accessible to everyone, some Buddhists will agree that everybody can become enlightened.

_____

_____

_____

_____

_____

_____

_____

_____

_____

_____

5 'The witnessing of the four sights is the most important part of the Buddha's life.'

Evaluate this statement.

In your answer you should:

- refer to Buddhist teaching
- give reasoned arguments to support this statement
- give reasoned arguments to support a different point of view
- reach a justified conclusion.

[12 marks]
[SPaG 3 marks]

(!) REMEMBER...

- Focus your answer on the statement you are asked to evaluate. Do not include irrelevant information, views from other religions or non-religious views.

- Try to write at least three paragraphs – one with arguments to support the statement, one with arguments to support a different point of view, and a final paragraph with a justified conclusion stating which side you think is more convincing, and why.

- Make sure you fully develop your points with evidence that includes teachings from Buddhism.

- Include a justified conclusion where you make a judgement about which side is stronger based on the evidence you have discussed. You can use phrases such as 'I think this is a convincing argument because...'

6 'It is extremely difficult for Buddhists to follow the Eightfold Path today.'

Evaluate this statement.

In your answer you should:

- refer to Buddhist teaching
- give reasoned arguments to support this statement
- give reasoned arguments to support a different point of view
- reach a justified conclusion.

[12 marks]
[SPaG 3 marks]

OXFORD
UNIVERSITY PRESS

Great Clarendon Street, Oxford, OX2 6DP, United Kingdom

Oxford University Press is a department of the University of Oxford. It furthers the University's objective of excellence in research, scholarship, and education by publishing worldwide. Oxford is a registered trade mark of Oxford University Press in the UK and in certain other countries

British Library Cataloguing in Publication Data

Data available

978-0-19-844564-7

1 2 3 4 5 6 7 8 9 10

Paper used in the production of this book is a natural, recyclable product made from wood grown in sustainable forests.

The manufacturing process conforms to the environmental regulations of the country of origin.

Printed in India by Manipal Technologies Limited

Acknowledgements

We are grateful to the authors and publishers for use of extracts from their titles and in particular for the following:

Scripture quotations taken from the *Holy Bible, New International Version Anglicised*, Copyright © 1979, 1984, 2011 Biblica. Used by permission of Hodder & Stoughton Ltd, an Hachette UK company. All rights reserved. 'NIV' is a registered trademark of Biblica UK trademark number 1448790.; Excerpts from **The Connected Discourses of the Buddha: A New Translation of the Samyutta Nikaya**, translated by Bhikkhu Bodhi (Wisdom Publications, 2005). Copyright © 2000 by Bhikkhu Bodhi. Reproduced with permission from The Permissions Company, Inc., on behalf of Wisdom Publications, www.wisdompubs. org.; Excerpts from **The Word of the Doctrine: Translation of Dhammapada**, translated by K.R. Norman, (Pali Text Society, 1997). Reproduced with permission from the Hon. Secretary, Pali Text Society.; **The Church of England:** *The Apostles' Creed*, https://www. churchofengland.org/our-faith/what-we-believe/apostles-creed#na (Archbishops' Council, 2019) © The Archbishops' Council, reproduced with permission.; **His Holiness Tenzin Gyatso the Dalai Lama:** tweet, Twitter, 2 March 2012, (Dalai Lama, 2012). Reproduced with permission from the Office of His Holiness The Dalai Lama.; **His Holiness Tenzin Gyatso the Dalai Lama:** prayer, Capitol Hill, Washington D. C., U.S.A., 7 March 2014, (Dalai Lama, 2014). Reproduced with permission from the Office of His Holiness The

Dalai Lama.; **His Holiness Tenzin Gyatso the Dalai Lama and J. Hopkins:** *How to Practice: the Way to a Meaningful Life*, with Jeffrey Hopkins (Atria Books, 2003). Copyright © 2001 by His Holiness The Dalai Lama and Jeffrey Hopkins. Reproduced with permission from Atria Books, a division of Simon & Schuster, Inc. All rights reserved.; **Sogyal Rinpoche:** *The Tibetan Book of Living and Dying*, edited by Patrick Gaffney & Andrew Harvey (Rider, 2008). © 1993 by Rigpa Fellowship. Reproduced with permission from Random House Group Ltd.; **A. Sumedho:** *The Four Noble Truths*, (Amaravati Publications, 1992). Reproduced with permission from Amaravati Publications.; **Thich Nhat Hanh:** *The Miracle of Mindfulness*, Preface and English translation by Mobi Ho (Rider, 2008). © 1975, 1976 by Thich Nhat Hanh. Preface and English translation Copyright © 1975, 1976, 1987 by Mobi Ho. Reproduced with permission from Beacon Press, Boston, Massachusetts and Penguin Random House LLC.

We have made every effort to trace and contact all copyright holders before publication, but if notified of any errors or omissions, the publisher will be happy to rectify these at the earliest opportunity.

Excerpts from **Dhammapada: Verses & Stories**, translated by Daw Mya Tin, M.A., (Pariyatti Publishing, 2019). Copyright holder not established at time of going to print.; Excerpts from **The Dhammapada: The Path of Perfection**, Penguin Classics, translated by Juan Mascaro, (Penguin Classics, 1973). Copyright holder not established at time of going to print.; Excerpts from **Karaniya Metta Sutta: The Discourse on Loving-kindness** (Sn 1.8), translated from the Pali by Piyadassi Thera, http://www.accesstoinsight.org/tipitaka/ kn/snp/snp.1.08.piya.html (Access to Insight (BCBS Edition), 2012). Copyright holder not established at time of going to print.; Excerpts from **Kodhavagga: Anger" (Dhp XVII)**, translated from the Pali by Acharya Buddharakkhita. http://www.accesstoinsight.org/tipitaka/ kn/dhp/dhp.17.budd.html (Access to Insight (BCBS Edition), 2013). Copyright holder not established at time of going to print.; Excerpts from **Kusala Sutta: Skillful" (AN 2.19)**, translated from the Pali by Thanissaro Bhikkhu. http://www.accesstoinsight.org/tipitaka/an/ an02/an02.019.than.html (Access to Insight (BCBS Edition), 2010). Copyright holder not established at time of going to print.; **Coventry Cathedral:** *Four Coventry Reflections on Reconciliation*, https://www. youtube.com/watch?v=FBYtcFSMNIU&t= (Coventry Cathedral, 2016). Copyright holder not established at time of going to print.; **His Holiness Tenzin Gyatso the Dalai Lama:** *The Art of Happiness: A Handbook for Living*, (Hodder & Stoughton, 1999). Copyright holder not established at time of going to print.

Cover: Peter Adams/Getty Images

Illustrations: Jason Ramasami and QBS Learning

Photos: p13: Renata Sedmakova/Shutterstock; **p.45 (L):** Mike Booth/ Alamy Stock Photo; **p.45 (R):** Monica Wells/Alamy Stock Photo; **p91:** NICK FIELDING/Alamy Stock Photo; **p103:** pema/Shutterstock; **p106:** I love photo/Shutterstock.

Although we have made every effort to trace and contact all copyright holders before publication this has not been possible in all cases. If notified, the publisher will rectify any errors or omissions at the earliest opportunity.

Links to third party websites are provided by Oxford in good faith and for information only. Oxford disclaims any responsibility for the materials contained in any third party website referenced in this work.

Please note that the practice questions in this book allow students a genuine attempt at practising exam skills, but they are not intended to replicate examination papers.

Thank you

OUP wishes to thank Matthew Narain, Aisha Mohammad and Julie Haigh for their help reviewing this book.